I0119623

Heinrich Preschers

The Gospel Temperance Hymnal and Coronation Songs

Heinrich Preschers

The Gospel Temperance Hymnal and Coronation Songs

ISBN/EAN: 9783743417724

Printed in Europe, USA, Canada, Australia, Japan

Cover: Foto ©Thomas Meinert / pixelio.de

More available books at **www.hansebooks.com**

THE

GOSPEL TEMPERANCE

HYMNAL

—AND—

CORONATION SONGS

A. S. BARNES & CO

NEW YORK AND CHICAGO

PREFACE.

———⟨∞⟩———

THIS little volume is issued with the hope that it may furnish the various temperance societies, and other bands of Christian workers, with a neat and inexpensive volume of good music for their regular meetings and for their more informal gatherings.

The aim has been to add many new pieces, and also to retain some of the time-honored old prayer-meeting hymns and tunes that awaken such memories of the time when we

> . . . . "fancied the Bethel-bent beam
> That trembled to earth in the Patriarch's dream,
> Was a ladder of song in that wilderness rest
> From the pillow of stone to the blue of the Blest,
> And the angels descending to dwell with us here,
> 'Old Hundred' and 'Corinth' and 'China' and 'Mear.'"

Care has been taken to select only such tunes as are within the scope of the ordinary voice ; it having been demonstrated that many more persons will join in congregational singing if the pieces sung do not require any great vocal effort.

It is earnestly hoped that this collection may contain some hymns and tunes that will touch responsive chords in many human hearts and be the means of doing a much greater good than simply aiding people in their "service of song."

INDORSEMENT.

HAVING examined the Hymns about to be published by Messrs. A. S. BARNES & Co., under the title of THE GOSPEL TEMPERANCE HYMNAL, I desire to give my approval to them, and to say that I believe this book, at the low price at which it is supplied, will prove a most valuable and efficient aid to our Christian workers.

Frances E. Willard.

EVANSTON, ILL., Jan'y 6th, 1886.

GOSPEL

TEMPERANCE HYMNAL.

No. 1.   JESUS, LOVER OF MY SOUL.

"The Lord will be a refuge in time of trouble."—PSALM 9 : 9.

Rev. CHARLES WESLEY.

S. B. MARSH.

1 { Je - sus, lov - er of my soul, Let me to Thy bo - som fly, }
{ While the near - er wa - ters roll, While the tempest still is high; }
D. C. Safe in - to the ha - ven guide, Oh, receive my soul at last.

Hide me. O my Saviour hide, Till the storm of life is past:

2 Other refuge have I none.
  Hangs my helpless soul on Thee;
Leave, oh. leave me not alone,
  Still support and comfort me.
All my trust on Thee is stayed ;
  All my help from Thee I bring ;
Cover my defenceless head
  With the shadow of Thy wing.

3 Thou, O Christ. art all I want;
  More than all in Thee I find:
Raise the fallen, cheer the faint.
  Heal the sick, and lead the blind.

Just and holy is Thy Name.
  I am all unrighteousness:
Vile, and full of sin I am,
  Thou art full of truth and grace.

4 Plenteous grace with Thee is found—
  Grace to cover all my sin :
Let the healing streams abound;
  Make me, keep me. pure within.
Thou of life the Fountain art,
  Freely let me take of Thee;
Spring Thou up within my heart,
  Rise to all eternity.

NEAR THE CROSS.

" Peace through the blood of His cross."—COLL. 1: 29.

FANNY J. CROSBY.

W. H. DOANE, by per.

1. Je - sus, keep me near the cross,   There a pre - cious fountain
2. Near the cross, a trembling soul,   Love and mer - cy found me;
3. Near the cross! O Lamb of God,   Bring its scenes be - fore me;
4. Near the cross I'll watch and wait,   Hop - ing, trust - ing ev - er,

Free to all-- a heal - ing stream, Flows from Calvary's mountain.
There the bright and morn-ing star Shed its beams a - round me.
Help me walk from day to day With its shad - ows o'er me.
Till I reach the gold - en strand Just be - yond the riv - er.

Chorus.

In the cross, in the cross Be my glo - ry ev - er;

Till my rap - tured soul shall find Rest be-yond the riv - er.

BRINGING IN THE SHEAVES.

"The harvest is the end of the world."—MATT. 13: 39.

KNOWLES SHAW.　　　　　　　　　　　GEORGE A. MINOR, by per.

1. Sow-ing in the morn-ing, sow-ing seeds of kind-ness, Sowing in the
2. Sow-ing in the sun-shine, sow-ing in the shad-ows, Fearing neither
3. Go-ing forth with weep-ing, sow-ing for the Mas-ter, Tho' the loss sus-

noon-tide and the dew-y eve; Wait-ing for the har-vest, and the
clouds nor win-ter's chill-ing breeze; By and by the har-vest, and the
tain'd our spir-it oft-en grieves; When our weeping's o-ver, He will

time of reap-ing, We shall come, re-joic-ing, bringing in the sheaves.
la-bor end-ed, We shall come, re-joic-ing, bringing in the sheaves.
bid us wel-come, We shall come, re-joic-ing, bringing in the sheaves.

Chorus.

Bringing in the sheaves, bringing in the sheaves, We shall come, re-joic-

1 -ing, bring-ing in the sheaves, 2 -ing, bring-ing in the sheaves.

I NEED THE PRAYERS OF THOSE I LOVE.

No. 4.

"Prayer was made without ceasing of the church unto God for him"—Acts 12:5.

J. E. RANKIN, D.D.

E. S. LORENZ.

1. I need the prayers of those I love! I need the sweet, sweet feeling, That suit for me is urged a-bove, When-e'er dear friends are kneel-ing.

A - mid life's cares I need the prayers I

A - mid life's cares I need the prayers,

need the prayers of those I love A -

I need the prayers of those I love, of those I love.

- mid life's cares I need the prayers I

A - mid life's cares, I need the prayers

I NEED THE PRAYERS.—Concluded.

need the prayers........... of those I love...............

I need the prayers of those I love, of those I love.

2 Of those I love the prayers I need !
They know my wants and ailings ;
They know the way to intercede
For all my faults and failings.
On bended knee,
Remember me,
Of those I love the prayers I need.

3 Of those I love, I need the prayers!
Whene'er God's throne addressing:
'Twill keep my feet from sins and snares,
'Twill break in show'rs of blessing,
Who love me yet,
O ne'er forget ;
Of those I love. I need the prayers!

No. 5. WILL YOU MEET US ?

ANON.   Slave Melody.

1. Say, brothers, will you meet us, Say, brothers, will you meet us,

Say, brothers, will you meet us, On Ca-naan's hap - py shore?

2 Say, sisters, will you meet us
On Canaan's happy shore ?

3 By the grace of God I'll meet you
On Canaan's happy shore.

4 That will be a happy meeting
On Canaan's happy shore.

5 Jesus lives and reigns forever
On Canaan's happy shore.

No. 7.   CLOSE TO THEE.

FANNY J. CROSBY.

S. J. VAIL, by per.

1. Thou, my ev - er - last - ing por-tion, More than friend or life to me,
2. Not for ease or world - ly pleasure, Nor for fame my prayer shall be;
3. Lead me thro' the vale of shadows, Bear me o'er life's fit - ful sea:

All a-long my pil-grim jour - ney, Sav - iour, let me walk with Thee.
Glad - ly will I toil and suf - fer, On - ly let me walk with Thee.
Then the gate of life e - ter - nal May I en - ter, Lord, with Thee.

Chorus.

Close to Thee, close to Thee, Close to Thee, close to Thee; All a-
Close to Thee, close to Thee, Close to Thee, close to Thee; Glad - ly
Close to Thee, close to Thee, Close to Thee, close to Thee; Then the

long my pil - grim jour - ney, Sav - iour, let me walk with Thee.
will I toil and suf - fer, On - ly let me walk with Thee.
gate of life e - ter - nal May I en - ter, Lord, with Thee.

(10)

ALAS! AND DID MY SAVIOUR BLEED?

No. 8. "He was wounded for our transgressions."—Is. 53 : 5.

I. WATTS. 1707.

S. J. VAIL.

1. A - las! and did my Sa-viour bleed? And did my Sovereign die?
2. Was it for crimes that I have done? He groan'd up-on the tree?
3. Well might the sun in dark-ness hide, And shut his glo - ries in,

Would He de -vote that sa - cred head For such a worm as I?
A - maz - ing pi - ty! grace unknown! And love be-yond de - gree!
When Christ, the migh -ty Mak - er, died For man the crea-ture's sin.

Chorus.

Je - sus died for you, Je - sus died for me,
for me,
for you,

Yes, Je - sus died for all man-kind, Bless God, sal - va - tion's free.

4 Thus might I hide my blushing face
   While His dear cross appears,
   Dissolve my heart in thankfulness,
   And melt mine eyes to tears.

   CHO:—Jesus died for you, &c.

5 But drops of grief can ne'er repay
   The debt of love I owe:
   Here, Lord, I give myself away;
   'Tis all that I can do.

   CHO: Jesus died for you, &c.

By Permission.

(11)

"TITLE CLEAR."

"Stand, therefore."—Eph. 12: 14.

Rearranged, with Chorus, by T. C. O'Kane.

1. When I can read my ti-tle clear, ti-tle clear, To mansions in the
2. Should earth against my soul en-gage, soul en-gage. And fie-ry darts be
3. Let cares, like a wild deluge come, deluge come, Let storms of sor-row
4. There I shall bathe my wea-ry soul, wea-ry soul, In seas of heav'nly

skies, in the skies, I'll bid fare-well to ev-ery fear,
hurled, darts be hurled, Then I can smile at Sa-tan's rage,
fall, sor-row fall, So I but safe-ly reach my home,
rest, heavenly rest, And not a wave of trou-ble roll

Chorus.

And wipe my weep-ing eyes. We will stand the
And face a frowning world. We will stand, stand the storm, It will
My God, my heaven. my all. A-cross my peace-ful breast.

storm, . . . We will an - chor by - and
not be ver - y long, We will an-chor by-and-by, We will

TITLE CLEAR.—Concluded.

by, by - and - by, We will stand . . . the
an - chor by - and - by, We will stand, stand the storm, It will

storm, . . . We will an - chor by - and - by, by - and - by.
not be ver - y long, We will an - chor by - and - by, by - and - by.

No. 10. DEPTH OF MERCY.

"A broken and a contrite heart, O God, thou wilt not despise."—Psa. 51: 17.

Rev. Chas. Wesley.   J. Stevenson.

1. { Depth of mer - cy, can there be   Mer - cy still reserved for me? }
{ Can my God His wrath for - bear,   Me, the chief of sin ners spare? }

Chorus.   *Smoothly.*   *Repeat pp*

{ God is love, I do believe: }
{ He is waiting to forgive, } He is waiting, waiting to for - give.

2 I have long withstood His grace;
Long provoked Him to His face;
Would not harken to His calls;
Grieved Him by a thousand falls.
Cho:—God is love, &c.

3 Now incline me to repent:
Let me now my sins lament;
Now my foul revolt deplore,
Weep, believe, and sin no more.
Cho:— God is love, &c.

No. 11. REJOICE AND BE GLAD.

Rev. HORATIUS BONAR, 1874. English Melody.

1. Re-joice and be glad! The Re-deem-er has come! Go look on His

Chorus.

cra-dle, His cross, and His tomb. Sound His praises, tell the Sto-ry Of

Cho. for 7th verse.—Sound His praises, tell the Sto-ry Of

Him who was slain; Sound His praises, tell with gladness, He liv-eth a-gain.

Him who was slain; Sound His praises, tell with gladness, He cometh a-gain.

2 Rejoice and be glad!
  It is sunshine at last!
  The clouds have departed,
  The shadows are past.—*Cho.*

3 Rejoice and be glad!
  For the blood hath been shed;
  Redemption is finished,
  The price hath been paid.—*Cho.*

4 Rejoice and be glad!
  Now the pardon is free!
  The Just for the unjust
  Has died on the tree.—*Cho.*

5 Rejoice and be glad!
  For the Lamb that was slain,
  O'er death is triumphant,
  And liveth again.--*Cho.*

6 Rejoice and be glad!
  For our King is on high,
  He pleadeth for us on
  His throne in the sky.—*Cho.*

7 Rejoice and be glad!
  For He cometh again;
  He cometh in glory,
  The Lamb that was slain.—*Cho.*

No. 12. REVIVE US AGAIN.

1 We praise Thee, O God! for the Son of Thy love,
  For Jesus who died, and is now gone above.
Cho.—Hallelujah! Thine the glory, Hallelujah! amen,
  Hallelujah! Thine the glory, revive us again.

2 We praise Thee, O God! for Thy Spirit of light,
  Who has shown us our Saviour, and scattered our night.— *Cho.*

3 All glory and praise to the Lamb that was slain,
  Who has borne all our sins, and cleansed every stain.—*Cho.*

4 All glory and praise to the God of all grace,
  Who has bought us, and sought us, and guided our ways.—*Cho.*

5 Revive us again; fill each heart with Thy love,
  May each soul be kindled with fire from above.—*Cho.*

Rev. WM. PATON MACKEY, 1866

No. 13. GATHER THE HARVEST IN.

"The harvest truly is plenteous, but the laborers are few."—MATT. 9 : 37.

S. J. G.

ARR. from Rev. S. J. GRAHAM.

1. Be-hold! with grain the fields are white, Gather the har-vest in;
2. All ye who love the Mas-ter's cause, Gather the har-vest in;

Now it is day, soon comes the night; Gather the har-vest in.
Seek not to win the world's applause, Gather the har-vest in.

Chorus.

Gather the har - vest in...... Gather the har - vest in .....

Gather the harvest in,   Gather the harvest in,

Be-hold! the fields are al - read - y white, Gather the harvest in.

3 Ye noble servants of the Lord,
  Gather the harvest in;
And have your sheaves securely stored:
  Gather the harvest in.—*Cho.*

4 Then, when God's work on earth is done,
  The world redeemed from sin,
Ye all shall shine forth as the sun,
  The harvest gathered in. —*Cho.*

(15)

No. 14. PASS NOT BY.

Mrs. E. C. KINNEY.

T. E. PERKINS.

1. Je - sus, Sav - iour, hear our cry! Pass not by, oh, pass not by!
2. We have heard Thy footsteps near, Pass not by, oh, pass not by!
3. Prostrate in Thy path we lie— Pass not by, oh, pass not by!
4. Lord, we can - not let Thee go, Pass not by, oh, pass not by!

Thou art com - ing, Lord, so nigh, Bless us, too, oh, pass not by!
See the con - trite sin - ner's tear— Lis - ten to the long - ing sigh:
Lest our ver - y faith should die, Pass not by, oh, pass not by!
In our midst Thy presence show, Till Thou bless us will we cry:

Lord, ful - fil Thy presence now; Pour Thy Spir - it while we bow;
Je - sus, hear our earn - est call, Let Thy bless - ing rest on all;
To Thy gar - ments we will cling, All our need be - fore Thee bring;
Breathe, oh, breathe on us, we pray: Tar - ry not, oh, come to - day,

Turn to us, as one we cry, Pass not by, oh, pass not by!
When Thy Spir - it is so nigh, Pass not by, oh, pass not by!
Son of Da - vid, hear our cry, Pass not by, oh, pass not by!
While we wait, and watch, and cry, Pass not by, oh, pass not by!

Copyright, 1879, by Theodore E. Perkins.

(16)

No. 15. RATHBUN. 8s & 7s.

Sir John Bowring.

Ithamar Conkey.

1 In the cross of Christ I glory,
  Towering o'er the wrecks of time,
  All the light of sacred story
  Gathers round its head sublime.

2 When the woes of life o'ertake me,
  Hopes deceive and fears annoy,

Never shall the Cross forsake me;
  Lo! it glows with peace and joy.

3 When the sun of bliss is beaming
  Light and love upon my way,
  From the Cross the radiance streaming,
  Adds new luster to the day.

No. 16. ROCK OF AGES.

"The Lord is my defence, and my God is the Rock of my refuge."—Psa. 94: 22.

Rev. A. M. Toplady, 1776.

Dr. Thos. Hastings, 1839.

Fine.

1. Rock of A-ges, cleft for me, Let me hide my-self in Thee:
D.C.—Be of sin the doub-le cure, Save me from its guilt and power.

D.C.

Let the wa-ter and the blood, From Thy riv-en side which flowed,

2 Not the labor of my hands
  Could fulfil Thy law's demands;
  Could my zeal no respite know,
  Could my tears forever flow,
  All for sin could not atone;
  Thou must save, and Thou alone.

3 Nothing in my hand I bring,
  Simply to Thy cross I cling;
  Naked, come to thee for dress,

Helpless, look to Thee for grace;
  Foul, I to Thy fountain fly,
  Wash me, Saviour, or I die.

4 While I draw this fleeting breath,
  When mine eyes shall close in death,
  When I soar to worlds unknown,
  See Thee on Thy judgment throne,
  Rock of Ages, cleft for me,
  Let me hide myself in Thee.

(17)

TRUSTING IN THE PROMISE.

"He is faithful that promised."—HEB. 10 : 23.

Rev. H. B. HARTZLER.

E. S. LORENZ.

1. I have found re - pose for my wea - ry soul, Trust-ing in the
2. I will sing my song as the days go by, Trust-ing in the
3. Oh, the peace and joy of the life I live, Trust-ing in the

prom - ise of the Sav - ior; And a har - bor safe when the
prom - ise of the Sav - ior; And re - joice in hope, while I
prom - ise of the Sav - ior; Oh, the strength and grace on - ly

bil - lows roll, Trust-ing in the prom-ise of the Sav - ior. I will
live or die, Trust-ing in the prom-ise of the Sav - ior. I can
God can give, Trust-ing in the prom-ise of the Sav - ior. Who-so-

fear no foe in the dead-ly strife, Trust-ing in the prom-ise of the
smile at grief, and a - bide in pain, Trust-ing in the prom-ise of the
ev - er will may be saved to - day, Trust-ing in the prom-ise of the

Sav - ior; I will bear my lot in the toil of life, Trust-ing in the
Sav - ior; And the loss of all shall be high-est gain, Trust-ing in the
Sav - ior; And be - gin to walk in the ho - ly way, Trust-ing in the

prom - ise of the Sav - ior.

Refrain.

Rest-ing on His might-y arm for-ev - er, Nev - er from His lov - ing heart to sev - er, I will rest by grace In His strong embrace, Trusting in the prom-ise of the Sav-ior.

---

18. **PLEYEL'S HYMN.**

7s.

1 Brother, hast thou wandered far
  From thy Father's happy home,
With thyself and God at war?
  Turn thee, brother; homeward come.

2 Hast thou wasted all the powers
  God for noble uses gave?
Squandered life's most golden hours?
  Turn thee, brother ; God can save.

3 He can heal the deepest wound,
  He thy gentlest prayer can hear;
Seek Him, for He may be found;
  Call upon Him ; He is near.

Rev. J. F. CLARKE.

(19)

WHITE AS SNOW.

"Though your sins be as scarlet, they shall be as white as snow."—ISA. 1: 18.

J. H. TENNEY.

1. "White as snow!" can my trans-gres-sions Thus be whol-ly wash'd a-
2. "White as snow!" O, what a prom-ise For the heav-y-lad-en
3. Yes, at once, and that com-plete-ly, Thro' the blood of Christ, I

way! Leav-ing not a trace be-hind them, Like a cloud-less sum-mer day.
breast! When by faith the soul re-ceives it, Wea-ri-ness is chang'd to rest.
know All my sins, tho' red like crim-son, May be-come as white as snow.

"White as snow!"   "White as snow!"

"White as snow!"   "White as snow!" Je-sus cleanses white as

snow!" Tho' your sins be red like crim-son, They shall be as white as snow.

By Permission.   (20)

MY MISSION FIELD.

"Lord, what wilt Thou have me to do?"—ACTS 9 : 6.

T. CORBEN, D.D.

E. S. LORENZ.

1. I have oft sought to know, Where the Lord would have me go; I've
2. I am watch-ing to see If He's a-ny work for me: What-
3. Glad the sick - le I'd wield, How-so - ev - er rough the field, And

sought it up - on my knee. 'Tis my one great care, That He would hear my
ev - er that work may be: O would He but say This is the cho - sen
bar - ren the soil might be: I should be con - tent If with me, He but

D.S.—*'Tis my one great care, That He would hear my*

Chorus.

Fine.

prayer: I would go, where He lead - eth me.   I would go...... where He
way: I would go, where He lead - eth me.
went: I would go, where He lead - eth me.   I would go,   where

prayer: I would go, where He lead - eth me.

D.S.

lead - eth me,   I would go,.......... where He lead - eth me.
He lead-eth me,   I would go   where He lead-eth me.

Music by permission.   (21)

No. 21.

JESUS, MY ALL.

FANNY J. CROSBY.

ARR. by THEO. E PERKINS.

1. Lord, at Thy mer - cy - seat, Hum - bly I fall;
2. Tears of re - pent - ant grief Si - lent - ly fall;
3. Hark! how the words of love Ten - der - ly fall,
4. Still at Thy mer - cy - seat, Hum - bly I fall;

Plead - ing Thy prom - ise sweet, Lord, hear my call;
Help Thou my un - be - lief, Hear Thou my call;
Ere to the realms a - bove, Heard is my call;
Plead - ing Thy prom - ise sweet, Heard is my call;

Now let Thy work be - gin, Oh, make me pure with - in,
Oh, how I pine for Thee! 'Tis all my hope and plea:
Now ev - 'ry doubt has flown, Bro - ken my heart of stone,
Faith wings my soul to Thee, This all my hope shall be,

Cleanse me from ev - 'ry sin, Je - sus, my all.
Je - sus has died for me; Je - sus, my all.
Lord, I am Thine a - lone, Je - sus, my all.
Je - sus has died for me, Je - sus, my all.

(22

WHAT A FRIEND WE HAVE IN JESUS.

No. 22. "There is a Friend that sticketh closer than a brother."—
PROV. 18 : 24.

REV. H. BONAR.

CHARLES C. CONVERSE.

1. What a friend we have in Je - sus, All our sins and griefs to bear;
2. Have we tri - als and temp-ta-tions? Is there trouble a - ny-where?
3. Are we weak and heav-y la - den, Cumbered with a load of care?

What a priv - i - lege to car - ry Ev - ery thing to God in prayer.
We should nev - er be discouraged, Take it to the Lord in prayer.
Pre - cious Saviour, still our refuge,— Take it to the Lord in prayer.

Oh, what peace we oft - en for - feit, Oh, what needless pain we bear—
Can we find a Friend so faith - ful, Who will all our sorrows share?
Do thy friends despise, for - sake thee? Take it to the Lord in prayer;

All because we do not car - ry Ev - ery thing to God in prayer.
Je - sus knows our ev - ery weakness, Take it to the Lord in prayer.
In His arms He'll take and shield thee, Thou wilt find a so - lace there.

MORE LOVE TO THEE.

Mrs. Prentiss

Theo. E. Perkins

1. More love to Thee, O Christ! More love to Thee! Hear Thou the pray'r I make
2. Once earthly joy I craved, Sought peace and rest; Now Thee a - lone I seek,
3. Let sorrow do its work, Send grief and pain ; Sweet are Thy mes-sen-gers,

On bend- ed knee ; This is my earn-est plea, More love, O)
Give what is best : This all my pray'r shall be, More love, O }
Sweet their re - frain, When they can sing with me, More love, O)

Christ! to Thee, More love, O Christ! to Thee, More love to Thee.

No. 23½. EVEN ME.

Mrs. Codner.

Theo. E. Perkins.

1. Lord, I hear of show'rs of blessings Thou art scatt'ring full and free;
2. Pass me not, O God, our Fa - ther! Sin - ful tho' my heart may be;
3. Pass me not, O gracious Sav-iour! Let me live and cling to Thee!

Show'rs the thirst-y land re-fresh-ing, Let some droppings fall on me—
Thou might's leave me, but the rath-er Let Thy mer - cy fall on me—
For I'm long-ing for Thy fa - vor; Whilst thou'rt calling, call on me—

4 Pass me not, O mighty Spirit,
Thou canst make the blind to see;
Testify of Jesus' merit!
Speak some word of power to me!
Even me, even me!
Speak some word of power to me.

5 Love of God—so pure and changeless,
Blood of Christ—so rich, so free;
Grace of God—so strong and boundless,
Magnify it all in me!
Even me, even me!
Magnify it all in all!

No. 24. HAMBURG. L. M.

1. Just as I am with-out one plea, But that Thy blood was shed for me,
2. Just as I am, and wait-ing not To rid my soul of one dark blot,
3. Just as I am, tho' tossed a-bout With ma-ny a con - flict, ma-ny a doubt,
4. Just as I am, poor, wretched, blind, Sight, riches, heal - ing of the mind,

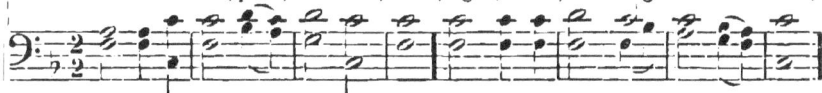

And that Thou bid'st me come to Thee, O Lamb of God! I come, I come.
To Thee, whose blood can cleanse each spot, O Lamb of God! I come, I come.
Fightings within, and fears without, O Lamb of God! I come, I come.
Yea, all I need, in Thee to find, O Lamb of God! I come, I come.

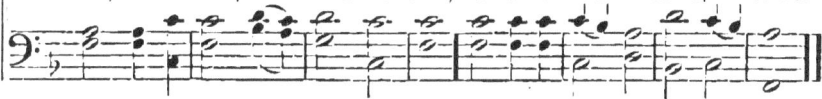

No. 25. THE SOLID ROCK.

L. M.   6 lines.

1 My hope is built on nothing less
Than Jesus' blood and righteousness;
I dare not trust the sweetest frame,
But wholly lean on Jesus' name:
On Christ, the solid rock, I stand;
All other ground is sinking sand.

2 When darkness seems to veil His face,
I rest on His unchanging grace;
In every high and stormy gale,
My anchor holds within the vail:
On Christ, the solid rock, I stand;
All other ground is sinking sand.

3 His oath, His covenant, and blood,
Support me in the whelming flood;
When all around my soul gives way,
He then is all my hope and stay;
On Christ, the solid rock, I stand,
All other ground is sinking sand.

Rev. EDWARD MOTE.

I LOVE TO TELL THE STORY.

No. 26. "I will speak of Thy wondrous work."—PSAL. 145: 5.

MISS KATE HANKEY, 1867.

W. G. FISCHER.

1. I love to tell the sto - ry Of unseen things above, Of Je - sus and His
2. I love to tell the sto - ry! More wonderful it seems, Than all the golden

Glo-ry Of Je - sus and His love! I love to tell the Sto - ry! Be-
fancies Of all our golden dreams. I love to tell the Sto - ry! It

cause I know it's true; It sat - is-fies my longings, As nothing else would do.
did so much for me! And that is just the reason, I tell it now to thee.

Chorus.

I love to tell the Sto - ry! 'Twill be my theme in glo - ry,

3 I love to tell the Story!
'Tis pleasant to repeat
What seems, each time I tell it,
More wonderfully sweet.
I love to tell the Story;
For some have never heard
The message of salvation
From God's own Holy Word.

4 I love to tell the Story!
For those who know it best
Seem hungering and thirsting
To hear it, like the rest.
And when, in scenes of glory,
I sing the NEW, NEW SONG,
'Twill be—the OLD, OLD STORY
That I have loved so long.

No. 27. THE WIDE, WIDE WORLD.

"The Lord alone did lead him."—DEUT. 32:12.

Rev. W. O. CUSHING.　　　　　　　　　　　　Rev. C. S. MEILY.

1. They tell me there are dan-gers In the path my feet must tread;
2. They tell me life has tri - als, And the fair - est hopes must flee;
3. I know my heart is sin - ful, And my love seems all too small;

But they can - not see the glo - ry That is shin-ing round my head.
But I trust my all in Je - sus, And I know He cares for me.
But if Je - sus' arm is round me I shall win and con - quer all.

D.S.—For I would not dare to jour-ney Thro' the wide, wide world a - lone.

Chorus.
D.S.

Oh, 'tis Je - sus leads my footsteps! He has made my heart His own:

From Heavenly Carols. By permission. (27)

IS IT THERE? WRITTEN THERE?

No. 28.   "Written in the Lamb's Book of Life."—Rev. 21 : 27.

J. E. Rankin, D.D.   E. S. Lorenz.

1. I do not ask for the pride of earth, For the pride of wealth, or the
2. I do not ask for a glo-rious name, That is writ-ten high on the
3. I do not ask that my earth-ly life Should be free from burdens, and
4. I'd give up all that I hope be-low, All that time can give, or the

pride of birth; Be this, the rath-er, my one great care: In the Book of
scroll of Fame: Be this, the rath-er, con-cern of mine, To in-sure it
cares and strife: Nor that its cur-rent have tranquil flow, If but this one
world be-stow, If when the Lord in His kingdom come, He will know me

Chorus.

Life, that my name is there. In the Book of Life, on those pa-ges fair,
there, in that Book di-vine.
thing, I may sure-ly know.
then, and will take me home.

Do the angels see that my name is there? In the Book of Life, on those p..-ges f..ir, Is it there? writ-ten there?

Is it there? writ-ten there!

No. 29. CORONATION. C. M.

Rev. EDWARD PERRONET.

OLIVER HOLDEN.

1. All hail the pow'r of Je - sus' name, Let an - gels pros-trate fall,
2. Crown Him, ye mar-tyrs of our God, Who from his al - tar call:

Bring forth the roy - al di - a - dem, And crown Him Lord of all,
Praise Him who shed for you His blood, And crown Him Lord of all.

Bring forth the roy - al dia - a - dem, And crown Him Lord of all.
Praise Him who shed for you His blood, And crown Him Lord of all.

3 Ye chosen seed of Israel's race,
Ye ransomed from the fall.
Hail Him who saves you by His grace,
And crown Him Lord of all.

4 Sinner! whose love can ne'er forget
The wormwood and the gall,
Go, spread your trophies at His feet,
And crown Him Lord of all.

5 Let every kindred, every tribe,
On this terrestrial ball,
To Him all majesty ascribe,
And crown Him Lord of all.

6 Oh, that, with yonder sacred throng,
We at His feet may fall:
We'll join the everlasting song,
And crown Him Lord of all.

ALL TO CHRIST I OWE.

Mrs. Elvina M. Hall.

John T. Grape, by per.

1. I hear the Sav-iour say, Thy strength in-deed is small;
2. Lord, now in-deed I find Thy pow'r, and Thine a - lone,
3. For noth - ing good have I Where - by Thy grace to claim—
4. When from my dy-ing bed My ran - somed soul shall rise,
5. And when be - fore the throne I stand in Him com-plete,

Child of weakness, watch and pray, Find in Me thine all in all.
Can change the lep-er's spot, And melt the heart of stone.
I'll wash my garment white In the blood of Calvary's Lamb.
Then "Je - sus paid it all" Shall rend the vault-ed skies.
I'll lay my trophies down, All down at Je - sus' feet.

Chorus.

Je - sus paid it all, All to Him I owe;

Sin had left a crim-son stain: He washed it white as snow.

No. 31.　THE GATE AJAR FOR ME.

Mrs. Lydia Baxter.　　　　　　　S. J. Vail, by per.　Philip Phillips.

1. There is a gate that stands a-jar, And, thro' its por-tals gleam-ing,
2. That gate a-jar stands free to all Who seek thro' it sal-va-tion;
3. Press onward, then, tho' foes may frown, While mercy's gate is o-pen,
4. Be-yond the riv-er's brink we'll lay The Cross that here is giv-en,

A radiance from the Cross a-far The Sav-iour's love re-veal-ing.
The rich and poor, the great and small, Of ev-'ry tribe and na-tion.
Ac-cept the cross, and win the crown, Love's ev-er-last-ing tok-en.
And bear the Crown of life a-way, And love Him more in heav-en.

Refrain.

Oh, depths of mer-cy! can it be That gate was left a-jar for me?

For me...... for me?...... Was left a-jar for me?
for me,　　　for me?

(31)

No. 32. THE GREAT PHYSICIAN.

"Is there no balm in Gilead; is there no physician there?"—JER. 8 : 22.

Rev. WM. HUNTER.   Arr. by Rev. J. H. STOCKTON.

1. The great Phy-si-cian now is near, The sym-pa-thiz-ing
2. Your ma-ny sins are all for-given. Oh, hear the voice of
3. All glo-ry to the dy-ing Lamb; I now be-lieve in

Je-sus: He speaks the drooping heart to cheer. Oh, hear the voice of
Je-sus: Go on your way in peace to heaven, And wear a crown with
Je-sus: I love the bless-ed Saviour's name, I love the name of

Chorus.

Je - sus.
Je - sus. "Sweetest note in ser-aph song, Sweetest name on
Je - sus.

mor-tal tongue. Sweetest car-ol ev-er sung, Je-sus, blessed Je-sus.

4 "The children too, both great and small,
  Who love the name of Jesus,
  May now accept the gracious call
  To work and live for Jesus."—Cho.

5 Come, brethren, help me sing His praise.
  Oh, praise the name of Jesus:
  Come, sisters, all your voices raise.
  Oh, bless the name of Jesus.—Cho.

6 His name dispels my guilt and fear,
  No other name but Jesus:
  Oh, how my soul delights to hear
  The precious name of Jesus.—Cho.

7 And when to that bright world above,
  We rise to see our Jesus,
  We'll sing around the throne of love
  His name, the name of Jesus.—Cho.

(32)

No. 33.   I AM PRAYING FOR YOU.

"Evening, and morning, and at noon, will I pray."—Psa. 55 : 17.

S. O'Maley Cluff.   Ira D. Sankey.

1. I have a Saviour, He's pleading in glo - ry, A dear, lov-ing Saviour tho'
2. I have a Fa-ther: to me He has giv-en A hope for e - ter - ni - ty.
3. I have a robe : 'tis re-splendent in whiteness, A-wait-ing in glo - ry my

earth-friends be few; And now He is watching in ten-der-ness o'er me. And
bless-ed and true; And soon will He call me to meet Him in heav-en, But
won - der-ing view; Oh, when I re - ceive it all shin-ing in brightness, Dear

Chorus.

oh that my Saviour were your Saviour too!
oh that He'd let me bring you with me too!   For you I am praying, For
friend, could I see you re-ceiv-ing one too!

you I am pray-ing, For you I am praying, I'm pray-ing for you.

4 I have a peace: it is calm as a river—
   A peace that the friends of this world never knew ;
   My Saviour alone is its Author and Giver,
   And oh, could I know it was given to you!—Cho.

5 When Jesus has found you, tell others the story,
   That my loving Saviour is your Saviour too ;
   Then pray that your Saviour may bring them to glory,
   And prayer will be answered —'twas answered for you!—Cho.

By permission.   (32)

THERE'S A BETTER TIME A-COMING.

No. 34.

Words and Music by
J. E. RANKIN, D.D.

Arr. by J. W.

1–5. There's a bet-ter time, a-coming, By and by, by

1. You can catch the glo-ry breaking In the sky, in the sky.
2. You can catch the glo-ry breaking In the sky, in the sky.
3. You can catch the glo-ry breaking In the sky, in the sky.
4. You can catch the glo-ry breaking In the sky, in the sky.
5. You can catch the glo-ry breaking In the sky, in the sky.

words which shall be spoken; Lov-ing hearts no more be broken:
more will tempt each oth-er; Sin-ful passions, they will smother;
wrongs, then, love shall right them, All men's battles, love shall fight them
true! we here declare it! We'll be loy-al! now we swear it!
Lord to go be-fore us, With His ban-ner float-ing o'er us,

Cross shall be the to-ken, Of the bet-ter time a-c
then, be true to brother, In the bet-ter time a-c
foes, we'll win de-spite them, In the bet-ter time a-c
need-ful, do or dare it. For the bet-ter time a-c
shout, we shout the cho-rus, Of the bet-ter time a-c

Chorus.

There's a bet-ter time coming By and by, By and by,

(34)

bet-ter time coming, By and by, By and by, There's a bet-ter time

com-ing, By and by, By and by, And you can help it on.

No. 35. NETTLETON. 8s & 7s.

Rev. R. Robinson, 1758.

Old Melody, 1812.

Fine.

1. { Come, Thou Fount of ev-er-y bless-ing, Tune my heart to sing Thy grace; }
   { Streams of mer-cy, nev-er ceas-ing, Call for songs of loud-est praise; }

D.C.—Praise the mount—I'm fixed up - on it! Mount of Thy re-deem-ing love.

D. C.

Teach me some me - lo-dious son-net, Sung by flam-ing tongues a-bove:

2 Here I'll raise my Ebenezer,
  Hither by Thy help I'm come:
  And I hope by Thy good pleasure,
  Safely to arrive at home.
  Jesus sought me when a stranger,
  Wandering from the fold of God;
  He to rescue me from danger,
  Interposed His precious blood.

3 Oh, to grace how great a debtor,
  Daily I'm constrained to be!
  Let Thy goodness as a fetter,
  Bind my wandering heart to Thee;
  Prone to wander, Lord I feel it —
  Prone to leave the God I love —
  Here's my heart, oh, take and seal it,
  Seal it for Thy courts above.

SHALL WE FIND THEM AT THE PORTALS?

"I shall go to him."—2 Sam, 12 : 16.

J. E. RANKIN, D.D.

E. S. LORENZ.

1. Will they meet us, cheer and greet us, Those we've lov'd, who've gone be-fo
2. Hearts are brok-en, for some tok - en, That they live and love us ye
3. And we of - ten, as days sof - ten, And comes out the even-ing sta
4. Past yon por - tals, our im-mor - tals, Those who walk with Him in whi

Shall we find them at the por-tals, Find our beau-ti - fied im-mor-ta
And we ask, " Can those who've left us, Of love's look and tone be - reft
Looking westward, sit and won-der, Whether, when so far a - sun-d
Do they, 'mid their bliss, re - call us? Know they what events be - fall u

D.S.—*We shall find them at the portals, Find our beau-ti - fied im-mor-t*

Chorus.

Fine.

When we reach that ra-diant shore? They will meet us, cheer a
Tho' in Heav'n, can they for - get?"
They still think how dear they are?
Will our com - ing wake de - light? They will meet us,

When we reach that ra-diant shore.

D.

greet us, Those we've lov'd, who've gone be - fore ;

cheer and greet us,

be-fore

(36)

No. 37. I HEAR THY WELCOME VOICE.

"Come unto Me, all ye that labor and are heavy-laden, and I will
give you rest."—MATT. 11: 28.

Rev. L. HARTSOUGH.

From "Hallowed Songs."

1. I hear Thy wel-come voice That calls me, Lord, to Thee For
2. Tho' com-ing weak and vile, Thou dost my strength as-sure; Thou
3. 'Tis Je-sus calls me on To per-fect faith and love, To
4. 'Tis Je-sus who con-firms The bless-ed work with-in, By

cleans-ing in Thy pre-cious blood That flowed on Cal-va-ry.
dost my vile-ness ful-ly cleanse, Till spot-less all and pure.
per-fect hope, and peace, and trust, For earth and heaven a-bove.
add-ing grace to welcomed grace, Where reigned the power of sin.

Chorus.

I am com-ing Lord! Com-ing now to Thee!

Wash me, cleanse me, in the blood That flowed on Cal-va-ry.

5 And He the witness gives
   To loyal hearts and free,
That every promise is fulfilled,
   If faith but brings the plea.

6 All hail, atoning blood!
   All hail, redeeming grace!
All hail, the Gift of Christ, our Lord,
   Our Strength and Righteousness!

By permission.

(37)

No. 38.　I NEED THEE EVERY HOUR.

"Without Me ye can do nothing."—JOHN 15: 5.

Mrs. ANNIE S. HAWKS.　　　　　　　Rev. ROBERT LOWRY, by per.

1. I need Thee ev - 'ry hour, Most gra - cious Lord;
2. I need Thee ev - 'ry hour; Stay Thou near by;
3. I need Thee ev - 'ry hour In joy or pain;
4. I need Thee ev - 'ry hour; Teach me Thy will;
5. I need Thee ev - 'ry hour, Most Ho - ly One;

No ten - der voice like Thine Can peace af - ford.
Temp - ta - tions lose their pow'r When Thou art nigh.
Come quick - ly and a - bide, Or life is vain.
And Thy rich prom - is - es In me ful - fil.
Oh, make me Thine in - deed, Thou bless - ed Son.

Refrain.

I need Thee, oh! I need Thee, Ev - 'ry hour I need Thee;

O bless me now, my Sav - iour! I come to Thee.

No. 39. HASTEN, LORD, THE GLORIOUS TIME.

HARRIET AUBER.

Dr. LOWELL MASON.

1. Has-ten, Lord, the glo-rious time, When, be-neath Mes- si - ah's sway,
2. Then shall wars and tu-mults cease, Then be banished grief and pain;

Ev - 'ry na - tion, ev - 'ry clime, Shall the gos - pel call o - bey.
Righteous-ness and joy and peace, Un-disturbed shall ev - er reign.

Mightiest kings His pow'r shall own, Heathen tribes His name a - dore;
Bless we then our gracious Lord; Ev- er praise His glorious name;
Mightiest kings Heathen tribes
Bless we then Ev-er praise

Sa - tan and his host, o'erthrown, Bound in chains, shall hurt no more.
All His might-y acts re - cord, All His wondrous love pro - claim.

THE LORD IS MY LIGHT.

The Lord is my light and my salvation; whom shall I fear? the Lord is the strength of my life; of whom shall I be afraid?—PSALMS, 27: 1.

Words by JAMES NICHOLSON. Music by J. W. BISCHOFF.

1. The Lord is my light, then why should I fear? By
2. The Lord is my light, though clouds may a - rise; Faith
3. The Lord is my light, the Lord is my strength: I
4. The Lord is my light, my all and in all; There

day and by night His presence is near; He is my sal - va - tion from
stronger than sight looks up to the skies; When Je - sus for ev - er in
know in His might I'll con-quer at length; My weakness in mer - cy He
is in His sight no darkness at all; He is my Re-deem - er, my

sor - row and sin; This blessed per - sua-sion the Spir - it brings in.
glo - ry doth reign, Then how can I ev - er in darkness re-main?
cov - ers with power, And walk-ing by faith He.... saves me each hour.
Sav - iour and King; With saints and with an - gels His prais-es I sing.

Chorus.

The Lord is my light, my joy and my song: By day and by

By permission.

THE LORD IS MY LIGHT.—Concluded.

night He leads me a-long, The Lord is my light, my

joy and my song, By day and by night He leads me a-long.

No. 41. I AM COMING TO THE CROSS.

"Him that cometh to Me I will in no wise cast out."—JOHN 6: 37.

Rev. WM. McDONALD.   WM. G. FISCHER, *by per.*

1. I am com-ing to the cross; I am poor, and weak, and blind; I am
Cho.—*I am trusting, Lord, in Thee, Blest Lamb of Cal - va - ry; Humbly*

count-ing all but dross, I shall full sal - va - tion find.
at Thy cross I bow, Save me, Je - sus, save me now.

Long my heart has sighed for Thee,
  Long has evil reigned within;
Jesus sweetly speaks to me.—
  "I will cleanse you from all sin.—Cho.

Here I give my all to Thee,
  Friends, and time, and earthly store:
Soul and body Thine to be,—
  Wholly Thine for evermore.—Cho.

4 In thy promises I trust,
  Now I feel the blood applied:
I am prostrate in the dust.
  I with Christ am crucified.—Cho.

5 Jesus comes! He fills my soul!
  Perfected in Him I am:
I am every whit made whole:
  Glory, glory to the Lamb.—Cho.

ART THOU READY?

J. W. SLAUGHENHAUPT.   "Art thou ready?"—MATT. 24 : 44.   E. S. LORENZ.

1. Soon the eve-ning sha-dows fall-ing Close the day of mor-tal life:
2. Soon the aw-ful trum-pet sound-ing Calls thee to the judgment throne
3. Oh, how fa-tal 'tis to lin-ger! Art thou read-y—read-y now?
4. Priceless love and free sal-va-tion Free-ly still are of-fered thee;

Soon the hand of death ap-pal-ling Draws thee from its wea-ry strife.
Now pre-pare, for love a-bound-ing Yet has left thee not a-lone.
Read-y should Death's i-cy fin-ger Lay its chill up-on thy brow
Yield no long-er to temp-ta-tion, But from sin and sor-row-flee.

Chorus.

Art thou rea-dy?.... art thou rea-dy?.... 'Tis the
Art thou ready? art thou ready?

Spir-it call-ing, why de-lay? Art thou rea-dy?....
Art thou rea-dy?

Art thou rea-dy?.... Do not lin-ger long-er, come to-day.
Art thou read-y?

By permission.   (42)

No. 43. SWEET BY-AND-BY.

"The ransomed of the Lord shall return and come to Zion with songs and everlasting joy upon their heads."—Isa. 35 : 10.

S. FILLMORE BENNETT.　　　　　　　　　　　　　　　　　　JOS. P. WEBSTER.

1. There's a land that is fair - er than day, And by faith we can see it a-
2. We shall sing on that beauti - ful shore The me - lo - di - ous songs of the
3. To our boun-ti - ful Fa - ther a - bove, We will of - fer our trib-ute of

far ; For the Fa-ther waits o - ver the way, To pre-pare us a
blest, And our spir-its shall sor - row no more, Not a sigh for the
praise, For the glo - ri - ous gift of His love, And the blessings that

Chorus.

dwelling place there.
blessing of rest. In the sweet by - and - by, We shall
hal - low our days.

In the sweet by-and-by,

meet on that beau-ti - ful shore, In the sweet by - and

by-and-by by-and-by, by - and

by, We shall meet on that beau - ti - ful shore.

by. by - and- by,

By permission O. Ditson & Co.

HOME OF THE SOUL.

Mrs. Ellen H. Gates.

From "Hallowed Songs," by per.

1. I will sing you a song of that beau - ti - ful land, The
2. Oh, that home of the soul in my vis - ions and dreams, Its
3. That un-change-a - ble home is for you and for me, Where
4. Oh, how sweet it will be in that beau - ti - ful land, So

far a - way home of the soul, Where no storms ev - er beat on the
bright, jas- per walls I can see; Till I fan - cy but thin - ly the
Je - sus of Naz - a - reth stands; The King of all kingdoms for
free from all sor - row and pain; With songs on our lips and with

glit - ter - ing strand, While the years of e - ter - ni - ty roll,
veil in - ter - venes Be - - tween the fair cit - y and me,
ev - er, is He, And He hold - eth our crowns in His hands,
harps in our hands To meet one an - oth - er a - gain,

While the years of e - ter - ni - ty roll; Where no storms ev - er
Be - tween the fair cit - y and me; Till I fan - cy but
And He hold- eth our crowns in His hands; The King of all
To meet one an - oth - er a - gain; With songs on our

beat on the glit-ter-ing strand, While the years of e - ter - ni - ty roll.
thin - ly the veil in - ter- venes Be - tween the fair cit - y and me.
king-doms for - ev - er, is He, And He hold-eth our crowns in His hands.
lips and with harps in our hands To meet one an - oth - er a - gain.

THE HOME OVER THERE.

"Oh that I had wings like a dove, for then would I fly away
and be at rest."—Psalm 55 : 6.

Rev. D. W. C. Huntington.   Tullius C. O'Kane.

1. Oh, think of the home over there. By the side of the river of light. Where the
2. Oh, think of the friends over there. Who before us the journey have trod. Of the

over there,

saints, all im-mor - tal and fair,   Are robed in their garments of white. over there.
songs that they breathe on the air, In their home in the pal-ace of God, over there.

Refrain.

O-ver there,   o-ver there,   Oh, think of the home over there.   Over
O-ver there,   o-ver there,   Oh, think of the friends over there, Over

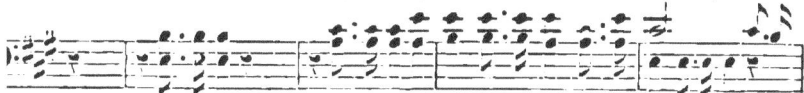

over there,   over there,   over there,

there,   o-ver there, o - ver there, Oh, think of   the home   o - ver there.
there,   o-ver there, o - ver there, Oh, think of   the friends o - ver there.

o-ver there,

3.
Saviour is now over there,
Where my kindred and friends are at rest;
Then away from my sorrow and care,
Let me fly to the land of the blest.
Over there, over there,
My Saviour is now over there.

4.
I'll soon be at home over there.
For the end of my journey I see ;
Many dear to my heart, over there,
Are watching and waiting for me.
Over there, over there,
I'll soon be at home over there.

By permission Philip Phillips.   (45)

No. 46. SAVED BY THE BLOOD OF JESUS.

"Which speaketh better things than the blood of Abel."—HEB. 12:

MAUD.

E.

1. Saved by the blood of Je - sus, Bro - ken the bonds o
2. Help - less and lone I wandered, Hope came to cheer n
3. Sing all ye saints in glo - ry, Sing ye redeemed b

Freed from the foes with - out us, Freed from the fears wit
Dark - ness was all a - round me, Crush - ing the load I
Tell, tell the old, glad sto - ry, Sweet - est that earth ca

Oh what a sweet sur - ren - der— Loss that is on - ly
Then gave I all to Je - sus, Sor - row, and sin an
Tell of His wondrous pit - y, Tell how He lived an

Oh what a bright glad dawn - ing, Af - ter sin's night of
Faith - ful and true and ten - der, Quick to my help H
Je - sus the earth-born Sa - viour, Je - sus the cru - ci

Chorus.

Saved by the blood of Je - sus, Bound by the love that free

(46)

more to roam — no more to roam, Oh wondrous love — oh rest and home.

WE PRAISE THEE, O GOD.

No. 47.

"O Lord, revive Thy work."—HAB. 3: 2.

1. We praise thee, O God! for the Son of Thy love, For..

Chorus.

Je - sus, who died, and is now gone a - bove. { Hal - le - lu - jah ! Thine the
{ Hal - le - lu - jah ! Thine the

glo - ry. Hal - le - lu - jah ! A - men. }
glo - ry. [OMIT.......................... } Re - vive us a - gain.

2 We praise Thee, O God! for Thy Spirit of light,
Who has shown us our Saviour, and scattered our night.

3 All glory and praise to the Lamb that was slain,
Who has borne all our sins, and has cleansed every stain.

4 All glory and praise to the God of all grace,
Who has bought us, and sought us, and guided our ways.

5 Revive us again; fill each heart with Thy love,
May each soul be rekindled with fire from above.

(47)

No. 48. WHY DO YOU WAIT?

"Arise, He calleth thee."—MARK 10: 49.

G. F. R.

GEO. F. ROOT, by per.

1. Why do you wait, dear broth- er, Oh, why do you
2. What do you hope, dear broth- er, To gain by a
3. Do you not feel, dear broth- er, His Spir - it now
4. Why do you wait, dear broth- er, The har - vest is

tar - ry so long? Your Sav - iour is wait - ing to
fur - ther de - lay? There's no one to save you but
striv - ing with - in? Oh, why not ac - cept His
pass - ing a - way, Your Sav - iour is long - ing to

give you A place in His sanc - ti - fied throng.
Je - sus, There's no oth - er way but His way.
- va - tion, And throw off thy bur - den of sin?
bless you, There's dan - ger and death in de - lay?

Chorus.

Why not? why not? Why not come to Him now? now?

(48)

No. 49. NEARER, MY GOD, TO THEE.

L. MASON.

1. Near - er, my God, to Thee, Near - er to Thee!
2. Though like the wan - der - er, The sun gone down,
3. There let the way ap - pear Steps un - to heaven;

E'en though it be a cross That rais - eth me;
Dark - ness be o - ver me, My rest a stone;
All that Thou send - est me, In mer - cy given;

Still all my song shall be, Near - er, my God, to Thee!
Yet in my dreams I'd be Near - er, my God, to Thee!
An - gels to beck - on me Near - er, my God, to Thee!

Near - er, my God, to Thee! Near - er to Thee!
Near - er, my God, to Thee! Near - er to Thee!
Near - er, my God, to Thee! Near - er to Thee!

4 Then with my waking thoughts
  Bright with Thy praise,
Out of my stony griefs
  Bethel I ll raise;
So by my woes to be
Nearer, my God, to Thee,
  Nearer to Thee !

5 Or if on joyful wing
  Cleaving the sky,
Sun, moon, and stars forgot,
  Upwards I fly,
Still all my song shall be,
Nearer, my God, to Thee,
  Nearer to Thee !

No. 50. TELL ME THE OLD, OLD STORY.

"Tell them how great things the Lord hath done."—MARK 5: 19.

Miss KATE HANKEY.   W. H. DOANE, by per.

1. Tell me the Old, Old Sto - ry, Of un.-seen things a - bove, Of
2. Tell me the Sto - ry slow - ly, That I may take it in— That

Je-sus and His glo - ry, Of Je- sus and His love. Tell me the Sto-ry
wonder-ful re - demp-tion, God's rem-e-dy for sin. Tell me the Sto-ry

sim-ply, As to a lit - tle child. For I am weak and wea - ry, And
oft - en, For I for - get so soon, The ear- ly dew of morn-ing Has

Chorus.

help-less and de - filed. } Tell me the Old, Old Sto-ry, Tell me the Old, Old
pass'd a - way at noon. }

Sto - ry, Tell me the Old, Old Sto - ry Of Je - sus and His love.

(50)

TELL ME THE OLD, OLD STORY.—Concluded.

3 Tell me the Story softly,
    With earnest tones, and grave;
    Remember! I'm the sinner
    Whom Jesus came to save.
    Tell me that Story always,
    If you would really be,
    In any time of trouble,
    A comforter to me.

4 Tell me the same Old Story.
    When you have cause to fear
    That this world's empty glory
    Is costing me too dear.
    Yes, and when that world's glory
    Is dawning on my soul,
    Tell me the Old, Old Story:
    "Christ Jesus makes thee whole."

No. 51. HE LEADETH ME.

"He leadeth me by the still waters."—PSALM 23: 2.

Rev. Jos. H. GILMORE. 1861.   WM. B. BRADBURY, by per.

1. He leadeth me! O blessed tho't! O words with heav'nly comfort fraught!
2. Sometimes 'mid scenes of deepest gloom, Sometimes where Eden's bowers bloom,
3. Lord, I would clasp Thy hand in mine, Nor ever mur- mur nor re- pine,
4. And when my task on earth is done, When, by Thy grace, the victory's won,

Whate'er I do, where'er I be, Still 'tis God's hand that leadeth me.
By wa- ters still, o'er troubled sea, Still 'tis His hand that leadeth me.
Content, whatev - er lot I see, Since 'tis my God that leadeth me.
E'en death's cold wave I will not flee, Since God thro' Jor- dan leadeth me.

Refrain.

He leadeth me! He leadeth me! By His own hand He leadeth me;
His faithful foll'wer I would be, For by His hand He lead-eth me.

(51)

GATHERING HOME.

MARY LESLIE.   W. A. OGDEN.

1. They're gath'ring homeward from ev'ry land, One by one,   one by one;

As their wea - ry feet touch the shining strand. Yes, one by one.

Their brows are enclosed in a gold - en crown, Their traveled-stain'd gar-

- ments are all laid down; And cloth'd in white raiment they rest in the mead. Where the

Lamb doth love His saints to lead. Gath'ring home, Gath'ring home, Fording the riv - er one by one; Gath'ring home, gath'ring home, Yes, one by one.

2 We, too, shall come to the river side,
   One by one, one by one;
We are nearer its waters each eventide,
   Yes, one by one;
We can hear the noise and the dashing stream,
Oft now and again through our life's deep dream;
Sometimes the dark floods all the banks overflow,
Sometimes in ripples and small waves go.

3 Jesus, Redeemer, we look to Thee,
   One by one, one by one;
We lift up our voices tremblingly,
   Yes, one by one;
The waves of the river are dark and cold,
We know not the place where our feet may hold;
O Thou who didst pass through in deepest midnight,
Now guide us, send us the staff and light.

No. 53.   TO-DAY.   6 & 4.

REV. S. F. SMITH.   DR. L. MASON, 1831.

1. To - day the Sav - iour calls: Ye wan- d'rers, come ; O,
2. To - day the Sav - iour calls: Oh, list - en now; With-

ye be - nighted souls, Why long- er roam?
in these sa - cred walls To Je - sus bow.

3 To-day the Savior calls :
   For refuge fly ;
The storm of justice falls,
   And death is nigh.

4 The Spirit calls to-day ;
   Yield to His power ;
Oh, grieve Him not away ;
   'Tis mercy's hour.

No. 54. ON THE SHOALS.

MARY B. REESE.   "Come, and help us."—ACTS. 16: 9.   T. C. O'KANE.

1. A cry comes o - ver the deep, Wailing of dy - ing souls, 'Ti
2. Sweet hope went out with the day, Rudder and compass lost; Do
3. Quick! point to the sav - ing Rock Looming from out the deep, Who.

echoed in ev - 'ry heart, "Brothers are on the shoals!" Th
spair more dark than night, Crowneth the tem - pest - tossed; No
bea-con the per - il'd soul? Ev - er will safe - ly keep, No

breakers are dash - ing high, And death is in ev - 'ry wave, An
help may come from the sea, No suc - cor from the land, Say
mat - ter how fierce the storm— How mad - ly the bil - low rolls, The

wild - ly ringeth the cry, "We perish. with none to save."
must they per - ish, and we Reach nev - er to them a hand?
light of the Guid - ing Star, Will bring them off the shoals.

Chorus. TRACE.

Ring out the tide of song, While prayer its bur-den rolls, Tha
of song,

From Jasper and Gold. By permission.   (54)

ON THE SHOALS.—Concluded.

He who rules the storm...... Will bring them off the shoals.

No. 55. **NO CROSS FOR ME?**

"They found a man, Simon by name, to bear the cross."—Matt. 27: 32.

T. CORBEN, D.D.   E. S. LORENZ.

1. Is there no cross for me, Thou dy-ing Lamb? Transfixed, Thy
2. Is there no cross for me, Thou stricken One? Who stretched Thee
3. Is there no cross for me, Ah! bless-ed Lord, How could there
4. Is there no cross for me, No fear, no frown, No blood, no

grief I see, Hard as I am. That suffering form of Thine;
to the tree? What had'st thou done? And why this crim-son tide,
glo-ry be, Or long re-ward; Thy joy, how. then, my own?
ag-o-ny, Ah! then, no crown, For rest comes out of strife;

That ag-o-ny di-vine! No cross for me, No cross for me?
Which wells forth from Thy side? No cross for me, No cross for me?
A seat up-on Thy throne. No cross for me, No cross for me?
And death comes out of life, No cross for me, No cross for me?

From *Praise Offering*. By per.   (55)

REST, PILGRIM, REST.

Words arranged and Music by THEODORE E. PERKINS.

1. Rest in the shadow of the Rock, O pil-grim, Rest, pil-grim, rest;
2. Rest in the shadow of the Rock, O pil-grim, Rest, pil-grim, rest;

Night treads close up-on the heels of day, There is no
Worn by jour-ney are the wea-ry feet, Turn, now, O

oth-er rest-ing place this way, The Rock is near, The well is clear:
pil-grim, to this calm re-treat, O sweet-ly rest, By care oppressed,

Rest in the shadow of the Rock, O Pil-grim, Rest, Pil-grim, rest.
Rest in the shadow of the Rock, O Pil-grim, Rest, Pil-grim, rest.

3 Rest in the shadow of the Rock, O pilgrim,
Rest, pilgrim, rest;
They who slumber by the Rock so dear,
Wake rejoicing, for their home is near,
Beneath its shade
Thy bed is made:
Rest in the shadow of the Rock, O Pilgrim,
Rest, Pilgrim, rest.

(56)

FRANCIS RIDLEY HAVERGAL.   WM. G. FISCHER.

Slow & prayerfully.

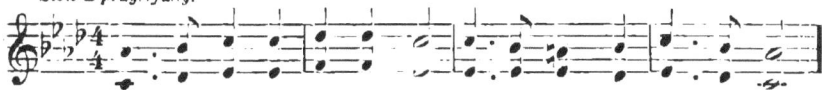

1. Take my life, and let it be Con - se - cra - ted, Lord, to Thee;
2. Take my feet, and let them be Swift and beau - ti - ful for Thee;
3. Take my sil - ver and my gold, Not a mite would I with-hold;
4. Take my will and make it Thine, It shall be no lon - ger mine;
5. Take my love; my Lord, I pour At Thy feet its treas - ure-store;

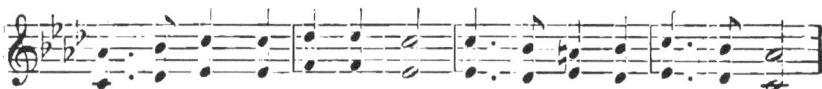

Take my hands, and let them move At the impulse of Thy love.
Take my voice and let me sing Al - ways, on - ly for my King.
Take my moments and my days, Let them flow in ceaseless praise.
Take my heart, it is Thine own, It shall be Thy roy - al throne.
Take my - self, and I will be Ev - er, on - ly, all for Thee.

Chorus.

Wash me in the Saviour's precious blood, Cleanse me in its pu-ri-fying flood;

Lord, I give to Thee my life and all to be Thine henceforth, e-ter-nal-ly.

By permission.   (57)

No. 58. BATTLING FOR THE LORD.

THEODORE E. PERKINS.

Semi-Chorus.   **Chorus.**

1. We've list - ed in a ho - ly war, Battling for the Lord!
2. We've gird - ed on our ar - mor bright, Battling for the Lord!
3. We'll stand like he - roes on the field, Battling for the Lord!
4. Tho' sin and death our way op - pose, Battling for the Lord!
5. And when our glo - rious war is o'er, Battling for the Lord!

Semi-Chorus.   **Chorus.**

E - ter - nal life, our guid - ing star, Battling for the Lord!
Our Cap-tain's word our strength and might, Battling for the Lord!
And no - bly fight but nev - er yield, Battling for the Lord!
Thro' grace we'll con - quer all our foes, Battling for the Lord!
We'll shout sal - va - tion ev - er-more, Battling for the Lord!

Full Chorus.

We'll work till Je - sus comes, We'll work till Je - sus comes,

WHEN WE LOSE OUR DEAR ONES HERE.

No. 59.

Words and Music by J. E. RANKIN, D.D.

1. When we lose our dear ones here, Those in faith de-part-ed, Oft we shed the bit-ter tear, Oft are bro-ken-heart-ed, Oft are bro-ken-heart-ed.

2 But, we know they still are ours,
   Where death ne'er invadeth;
   Where the bloom leaves not the flow'rs,
   |: And where love ne'er fadeth. :|

3 To the hills we lift our eyes,
   Where there is no dying;
   Whence the streams of comfort rise,
   ||: All sure hearts supplying. :||

4 To our Heavenly Father's will,
   Make we full surrender;
   Poor, weak hearts be hush'd and still,
   ||: He is kind and tender. :||

5 What, in tears, we know not now,
   We shall know hereafter;
   To the Lord we meekly bow:
   ||: Grief shall change to laughter. :||

I'LL SING FOR JESUS.

*"—— to whom be praise and dominion forever and ever."—*1 Pet. 4 : 11.

Rev. T. C. Reade.

J. H. Anderson.

1. I'll sing for Je-sus while I've breath, I'll praise Him when I die;
2. When sink-ing un-der sin and grief, No oth-er help was nigh;
3. My troubled soul found sweet re-pose, While trusting in His blood,

His lov-ing-kind-ness af-ter death I'll her-ald thro' the sky.
'Twas Je-sus came to my re-lief, 'Twas He who heard my cry.
And from the depths of sin a-rose, To dwell with Christ in God.

Chorus.

Sweet Sav - iour mine, I'll sing of thy wondrous love; I'll
Sweet Sav-iour, Saviour mine, I'll sing of thy wondrous love, wondrous love, I'll

serve Thee still, And I'll praise Thee up a-bove.
serve, yes, I'll serve thee still, serve thee still, And I'll praise thee up a - bove, up above.

By permission.

(60)

No. 63. SLEEPING ON GUARD.

ARTHUR W. FRENCH.

FRANK H. DAVIS.

1. Out from the camp-fire's red glowing, Cheerfully shedding its light, On to the pickets we're go-ing, For the long watches of night. Let us be careful that slum-ber Press not our eye-lids too hard, Surely not one of our number

Chorus.

Must be found sleeping on guard. Yes, sleeping on guard, Sleeping on guard, Sleeping on guard, guard... No, surely not one of our number Must be found sleeping on guard.

2 Yonder, rum's camp-lights are burning,
 Hark to the revelry there!
Waiting the conflict returning,
 Scouts round us throng ev'rywhere;
We must be watchful and ready,
 See every entrance is barred,
Keeping our heads cool and steady,
 All is lost sleeping on guard.

3 Our aim is vigilance ever,
 We can allow no defeat,
True-hearted soldiers will never
 Way from their duty retreat;
Wary and watchful be keeping,
 Though the task be e'er so hard,
Knowing what dangers come creeping,
 When they are sleeping on guard.

From Temp. and Gospel Songs, by per. (63)

No. 64. SAVIOUR, LIKE A SHEPHERD.

"He leadeth me in the paths of righteousness."—Ps. 23 : 3.

S. WESLEY MARTIN.

1. Sav-iour, like a shepherd, lead us, Much we need Thy ten-der
2. We are Thine, do Thou befriend us, Be the guardian of our
3. Thou hast promised to re-ceive us, Poor and sin-ful tho' we

1. Sav-iour, like a shep-herd, lead us, Much we need Thy
2. We are Thine, do Thou befriend us, Be the guard - ian
3. Thou hast prom-ised to re-ceive us, Poor and sin - ful

care; In Thy pleas-ant pas-tures feed us,
way; Keep Thy flock, from sin de-fend us,
be Thou hast mer-cy to re-lieve us,

ten-der care; In Thy pleas - ant pas-tures feed us,
of our way; Keep Thy flock, from sin de-fend us,
tho' we be; Thou hast mer - cy to re-lieve us,

For our use Thy folds pre-pare.
Seek us when we go a-stray.
Grace to cleanse, and power to free.

Chorus.

For our use Thy folds pre-pare. Bless-ed Je - sus,
Seek us when we go a-stray.
Grace to cleanse, and power to free.

By permission.

SAVIOUR, LIKE A SHEPHERD.—Concluded.

bless - ed Je - sus! Thou hast bought us, Thine we are. Thine we are.
bless - ed Je - sus! Hear, O hear us when we pray. when we pray.
bless - ed Je - sus! Help us, help us turn to Thee. turn to Thee.

No. 65.   REVIVE THY WORK.

ALBERT MIDLANE.   "O Lord, revive Thy work."—HAB. 3: 2.   E. S. LORENZ.

1. Re - vive Thy work, O Lord! Thy might - y arm make bare ;
2. Re - vive Thy work, O Lord! Dis - turb this sleep of death;

Speak with the voice that wakes the dead, And make Thy peo - ple hear.
Quick - en the smoldering em - bers now, By Thy al - might - y breath.

D.S. The glo - ry shall be all Thine own, The bless-ing, Lord, be ours.

Refrain.

Re - vive, re - vive Thy work, O Lord! Oh, send re - fresh - ing showr's!

3 Revive Thy work, O Lord !
  Exalt Thy precious name,
And, by the Holy Ghost, our love
  For Thee and Thine inflame.

4 Revive Thy work, O Lord !
  And give refreshing showers;
The glory shall be all Thine own,
  The blessing, Lord, be ours.

(65)

GO, WASH IN THE STREAM.

R. TORREY, JR.   "A fountain is opened for sin."—ZECH. 16: 1.   I. BALTZALL.

1. I'll sing of that stream, of that beau - ti - ful stream, That flows thro' th
2. I'll sing of that stream, of that beau - ti - ful stream, Which gladdens th
3. I'll sing of that stream, of that beau - ti - ful stream, That fount God ha
4. I'll sing of that stream, of that beau - ti - ful stream, That fount that is

sweet Ca-naan Land: Its wa-ters gleam bright in their heav-en - ly light, An
ci - ty of God: It flows from the throne of the Fa - ther a - lone; An
open - ed for sin: That stream from His side who for sin-ners once died: He
flow - ing so free: I'll sing of that flood, which is crimsoned with blood, Fro

Chorus.

rip - ple o'er the gold - en sand. Go wash in that beau - ti - ful
spreads its sweet wa - ters a - broad.
healed, who but plun - ges there - in.
sin, that has cleansed e - ven me.   Wash in the

stream............ Go, wash in that beau-ti - ful stream,..............
beau - ti - ful stream,   Wash in the beau-ti-ful stream, Its

wa - ters so free, are flow-ing for thee; Go, wash in that beauti-ful stream.

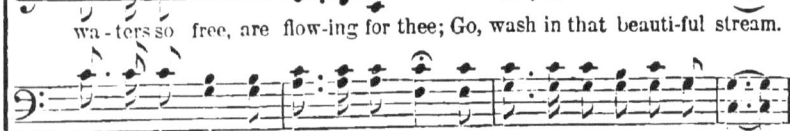

No. 67. SAFE WITHIN THE VAIL.

Rev. E. Adams.　　　　　　　　　　　　　　　J. M. Evans, by per.

1. "Land a - head!" its fruits are wav- ing O'er the hills of fade-less
2. On - ward bark! the cape I'm rounding; See the bless - ed wave their
3. There, "let go the an-chor," rid- ing On this calm and silv-'ry
4. Now we're safe from all temp-ta- tion, All the storms of life are

green; And the liv - ing wa-ters lav-ing Shores where heav'nly forms are seen.
hands; Hear the harps of God resounding From the bright immor-tal bands.
bay; Sea-ward fast the tide is gliding, Shores in sun-light stretch a-way.
past; Praise the Rock of our sal - va-tion, We are safe at home at last.

Chorus.

Rocks and storms I'll fear no more, When on that e- ter - nal shore; Drop the

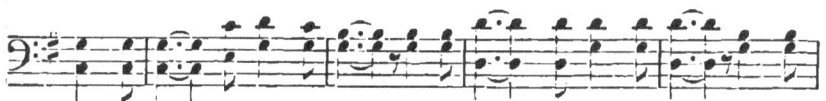

an - chor! Furl the sail! I am safe with- in the vail!

No. 68. SWEEPING THRO' THE GATES.*

"It is blood that maketh atonement for the soul."—Lev. 17 : 11.

T. C. O'K.   T. C. O'KANE.

1. Who, who are these be-side the chil-ly wave, Just on the bor-ders
2. These, these are they who in af-fliction's woes Ev - er have found in
3. These, these are they who in the con-flict dire, Bold-ly have stood a -
4. Safe, safe up-on the ev - er shining shore, Sin, pain, and death, and
5. May we, O Lord, be now en-tire-ly thine, Dai - ly from sin be

of the si-lent grave, Shouting Je - sus' pow'r to save, Wash'd in the blood
Je - sus calm re-pose, Such as from a pure heart flows, Wash'd in the blood
mid the hot-test fire; Je-sus now says, "Come up higher," Wash'd in the bloo
sor-row now are all o'er. Hap-py now and ev - er - more, Wash'd in the blood
kept by power di-vine; Then in heaven the saints we'll join, Wash'd in the bloo

Chorus.

of the Lamb? "Sweeping thro' the gates" to the New Je - ru - sa - lem,

"Wash'd in the blood of the Lamb........ "Sweep-ing thro' the gates
in the blood 'of the Lamb,

to the New Je - ru - sa - lem, "Wash'd in the blood of the Lamb."

By permission.   * Dying words of the Rev. Alfred Cookman.   (CC)

No. 69. JESUS, I MY CROSS HAVE TAKEN.

HENRY F. LYTE.　　　　　　　　　　　Air, MOZART. Arr. by H. P. M.

1. Je - sus, I my cross have taken, All to leave and fol - low Thee;
2. Let the world de-spise and leave me; They have left my Saviour, too;

Nak - ed, poor, despised, for-sak - en, Thou from hence my all shall be.

D.S.— Yet how rich is my con-di - tion! God and heav'n are still my own.
Hu- man hearts and looks deceive me; Thou art not, like them, untrue;
D.S.—Foes may hate, and friends may scorn me; Show Thy face and all is bright.

Per - ish ev - 'ry fond am-bi - tion, All I've sought, or hoped, or known;
And while Thou shalt smile upon me, God of wis-dom, love, and might,

3 Man may trouble and distress me,
　'Twill but drive me to Thy breast;
　Life with trials hard may press me,
　　Heaven will bring me sweeter rest.
　Oh! 'tis not in grief to harm me
　　While Thy love is left to me,
　Oh! 'twere not in joy to charm me,
　　Were that joy unmixed with Thee.

4 Soul, then, know thy full salvation;
　Rise o'er sin, and fear, and care,
　Joy to find in every station
　　Something still to do or bear.
　Soon shall close thy earthly mission,
　　Soon shall pass thy pilgrim days;
　Hope shall change to glad fruition,
　　Faith to sight, and prayer to praise.

No. 70. THE GOSPEL BELLS.

"For God so loved the world, that He gave His only begotten Son."—JOHN 3 : 16.

S. WESLEY MARTIN.   S. W. M.

1 The Gos-pel bells are ring-ing, O - ver land, from sea to sea:
2 The Gos-pel bells in - vite us To a feast pre-pared for all;
3 The Gos-pel bells give warn-ing, As they sound from day to day,
4 The Gos-pel bells are joy - ful, As they ech - o far and wide,

Bless-ed news of free sal - va - tion Do they of - fer you and me.
Do not slight the in - vi - ta-tion, Nor re - ject the gra-cious call.
Of the fate which doth a - wait them Who for - ev - er will de - lay.
Bear - ing notes of per - fect par-don, Thro' a Sav-iour cru - ci - fied.

"For God so loved the world That His on - ly Son He gave,
" I am the bread of life; Eat of me, thou hun-gry soul,
" Es - cape ye, for thy life; Tar - ry not in all the plain,
"Good tid - ings of great joy To all peo-ple do I bring,

THE GOSPEL BELLS.—Concluded.

Chorus.

Gos-pel bells, how they ring, O-ver land, from sea to sea; Golden

Gos-pel bells, how they ring,

bells, free-ly bring Bless-ed news to you and me.

Gold-en bells. free-ly bring

No. 71. AMERICA. 6s & 4s.

S. F. SMITH. H. CAREY.

1. My country, 'tis of thee, Sweet land of liberty, Of thee I sing; Land where my

fathers died, Land of the pilgrim's pride, From every mountain side Let freedom ring.

2 My native country, thee—
Land of the noble, free—
Thy name I love;
I love thy rocks and rills,
Thy woods and templed hills,
My heart with rapture thrills,
Like that above.

3 Our father's God, to Thee,
Author of liberty,
To Thee we sing—
Long may our land be bright
With freedom's holy light;
Protect us by Thy might,
Great God, our King.

No. 73. WE'LL WAIT TILL JESUS COMES.

Dr. MILLER, by per.

1. O land of rest, for thee I sigh, When will the moment come,
2. No tran-quil joys on earth I know, No peace-ful shelt'ring dome,

When I shall lay my ar-mor by, And dwell in peace at home?
This world's a wil-der-ness of woe, This world is not my home.

Chorus.

We'll wait till Je-sus comes, We'll wait till Je-sus comes,
We'll wait   We'll wait

We'll wait till Je-sus comes, And we'll be gath-ered home.
We'll wait

3 To Jesus Christ I fled for rest;
He bade me cease to roam,
And lean for succor on His breast,
And He'd conduct me home.

4 I sought at once my Saviour's side.
No more my steps shall roam:
With Him I'll brave death's chilling
And reach my heav'nly home. [tide

No. 74. THE PRODIGAL CHILD.

"I will arise, and go to my father."—LUKE 15: 18.

Mrs. ELLEN H. GATES.   W. H. DOANE.

1. Come home! come home! You are wea - ry at heart,
2. Come home! come home! For we watch and we wait,
3. Come home! come home! From the sor - row and blame,
4. Come home! come home! There is bread and to spare,

For the way has been dark, And so lone - ly and wild.
And we stand at the gate, While the shad - ows are piled.
From the sin and the shame, And the tempt - er that smiled;
And a warm welcome there; Then, to friends rec - on - ciled,

O prod - i - gal child! Come home! oh, come home!

Chorus.   *rit.*

Come home! Come, oh, come home!

By permission.
Come home, come home, come home!

(73)

THERE IS A FOUNTAIN.

WM. COWPER.   Western Melody.

1. There is   a fountain, fill'd with blood. Drawn from Immanuel's veins;
2. The dy - ing thief re-joiced   to see That fountain in his   day;

And sin-ners, plung'd be-neath that flood, Lose all their guil- ty stains.
And there may I, though vile as he, Wash all   my sins a - way.

Lose all   their guil - ty   stains,   Lose all their guilty stains, And
Wash all   my sins a - way,   Wash all my sins a - way, And

sin - ners, plung'd be-neath   that flood, Lose all   their guil-ty   stains.
there may I, though vile   as he, Wash all   my sins a - way.

3.
E'er since, by faith, I saw the stream
  Thy flowing wounds supply,
Redeeming love has been my theme,
  And shall be till I die.

4.
Then in a nobler, sweeter song,
  I'll sing Thy power to save, [tongue
When this poor, lisping, stammering
  Lies silent in the grave.

No. 76. WHAT MUST IT BE TO BE THERE?

"There shall be no more death, neither sorrow, nor crying."—REV. 21: 4.

Mrs. ELIZABETH MILLS.　　　　　　　　　　　GEO. C. STEBBINS, by per.

DUET.

1. We speak of the land of the blest, A
2. We speak of its path - ways of gold, Its
3. We speak of its peace and its love, The
4. We speak of its free - dom from sin, From
5. Do Thou, Lord, midst pleas - ure or woe, For

coun - try so bright and so fair, And oft are its
walls deck'd with jew - els so rare, Its won - ders and
robes which the glo - ri - fied wear, The songs of the
sor - row temp - ta - tion and care, From tri - als with-
heav - en our spir - its pre - pare, Then short - ly we

glo - ries con - fessed, But what must it be to be there?
pleas - ures un - told, But what must it be to be there?
bless - ed a - bove, But what must it be to be there?
- out and with - in, But what must it be to be there?
al - so shall know, And feel, what it be to be there.

Refrain.

To be there, to be there, Oh, what must it be to be there?

To be there, to be there, to be there?

To be there, to be there, Oh, what must it be to be there?

To be there, to be there, to be there?

(75)

IMMANNUEL'S LAND.

A. R. COUSIN.

WM. F. SHERWIN, by per.

1. The sands of time are wast - ing, The dawn of heav - en breaks,
2. Oh! Je - sus is the fount - ain, The deep, sweet well of love;
3. Oh! I am my Be - lov - ed's, And my Be - lov - ed's mine,

The sum - mer morn I've sigh'd for, The fair, sweet morn a - wakes.
The streams on earth I've tast - ed, More deep I'll drink a - bove.
He brings a poor vile sin - ner In - to his house di - vine.

Oh, dark hath been the mid - night, But day-spring is at hand,
There to an o - cean full - ness His mer - cy doth ex - pand,
Up - on the Rock of A - ges My soul redeemed shall stand,

And glo - ry, glo - ry dwell - eth In Im - man - uel's land,
And glo - ry, glo - ry dwell - eth In Im - man - uel's land,
Where glo - ry, glo - ry dwell - eth In Im - man - uel's land,

IMMANUEL'S LAND.—Concluded.

And glo-ry, glo-ry dwell-eth In Im-manuel's land.

No. 78.   BOYLSTON. S. M.

Rev. Isaac Watts.   Dr L. Mason.

1. Not all the blood of beasts On Jew-ish al-tars slain,
2. But Christ, the heav'n-ly Lamb, Takes all our sins a-way;

Could give the guilt-y conscience peace, Or wash a-way the stain.
A sac-ri-fice of no-bler name, And rich-er blood than they.

3 My faith would lay her hand
  On that dear head of thine,
While like a penitent I stand,
  And there confess my sin.

4 My soul looks back to see
  The burden thou did'st bear,
While hanging on the cursed tree,
  And knows her guilt was there.

————

1 Did Christ o'er sinners weep,
  And shall our cheeks be dry?

Let floods of penitential grief
Burst forth from every eye.

2 The Son of God in tears
  The wond'ring angels see;
Be thou astonish'd, O my soul;
  He shed those tears for thee.

3 He wept that we might weep;
  Each sin demands a tear:
In heaven alone no sin is found,
  And there's no weeping there.

(77)

No. 79. WHILE THE DAYS ARE GOING BY.

"Whatsoever thy hand findeth to do, do it with thy might."—Eccl. 9: 10.

GEORGE COOPER, by per.   IRA D. SANKEY.

1. { There are lone-ly hearts to cher-ish, While the days are go - ing by; }
   { There are wea-ry souls who per-ish, While the days are go - ing by; }
2. { There's no time for i - dle scorn-ing, While the days are go - ing by; }
   { Let your face be like the morn-ing, While the days are go - ing by; }
3. { All the lov-ing links that bind us, While the days are go - ing by; }
   { One by one we leave be - hind us, While the days are go - ing by; }

If a smile we can re - new, As our jour - ney we pur-
Oh, the world is full of sighs, Full of sad and weep-ing
But the seeds of good we sow, Both in shade and shine will

- sue, Oh, the good we all may do, While the days are go- ing by.
eyes; Help your fall - en brother rise, While the days are go- ing by.
grow, And will keep our hearts a-glow, While the days are go- ing by.

Refrain.

Go - ing by, go - ing by, Go - ing by, go - ing
Go-ing by, go-ing by, Go-ing by,

by, Oh, the good we all may do, While the days are going by.

go-ing by,   (78)

No. 80. THE STRANGER AT THE DOOR.

"If any man will open the door."—REV. 3 : 20.

T. C. O'KANE.

1. Be-hold a stran-ger at the door, He gently knocks—has knocked be-fore,
2. Oh, love-ly at-ti-tude He stands With melt-ing heart and load-ed hands;
3. But will He prove a friend indeed? He will—the ve-ry friend you need;

Has wait-ed long, is wait-ing still: You treat no oth-er friend so ill.
Oh, matchless kindness—and He shows This matchless kindness to His foes.
The Friend of sin-ners? Yes, 'Tis He, With garments dyed on Cal-va-ry.

Chorus.

Oh, let the dear Saviour come in.... He'll cleanse the heart from sin....
come in,   from sin,

Oh, keep Him no more out at the door, But let the dear Saviour come in'....
come in.

4 Rise, touched with gratitude divine,
Turn out His enemy and thine—
That soul destroying monster, 'sin,—
And let the heavenly Stranger in.

5 Admit Him, ere His anger burn—
His feet, departed, ne'er return;
Admit Him, or the hour's at hand
You'll at His door rejected stand.

Music by permission.

(79)

ARE YOU COMING HOME TO-NIGHT?

Arranged.

James McGranahan, by per.

1. Are you com-ing Home, ye wand'rers, Whom Je-sus died to win,
2. Are you com-ing Home, ye lost ones? Be-hold your Lord doth wait:
3. Are you com-ing Home, ye guilt-y, Who bear the load of sin?

All foot-sore, lame, and wea-ry, Your gar-ments stain'd with sin?
Come, then no lon-ger lin-ger, Come ere it be too late;
Out-side you've long been stand-ing, Come now and vent-ure in;

Will you seek the blood of Je-sus To wash your gar-ments white?
Will you come and let Him save you? O trust His love and might;
Will you heed the Saviour's prom-ise, And dare to trust Him quite?

Rit..........

Will you trust His pre-cious promise, Are you com-ing Home to-night?
Will you come while He is call-ing, Are you com-ing Home to-night?
"Come un-to me," saith Je-sus, Are you com-ing Home to-night?

Chorus.

Are you com-ing Home to-night, Are you com-ing Home to-night,

Are you com-ing Home to Je-sus, Out of darkness in-to light?

ARE YOU COMING HOME TO-NIGHT? Concluded.

To your lov-ing, heav'nly Fa-ther, Are you com-ing Home to-night?

No. 82. SHINING SHORE. 8s & 7s. D.

DAVID NELSON.   GEO. F. ROOT.

1. My days are gliding swift-ly by, And I, a pil-grim stran-ger,
2. Our absent King the watchword gave: "Let ev-'ry lamp be burning;"
3. Should coming days be dark and cold, We will not yield to sor-row;
4. Let sorrow's rudest tempest blow, Each chord on earth to sev-er;

Would not de-tain them as they fly, Those hours of toil and dan-ger,
We look a-far a-cross the wave, Our dis-tant home dis-cern-ing.
For hope will sing, with cour-age bold, There's glo-ry on the mor-row.
Our King says Come, and there's our home, For-ev-er! O for-ev-er!

For, O, we stand on Jordan's strand, Our friends are passing o-ver; And

just be-fore, the Shining Shore We may al-most dis-cov-er.

ANTIOCH. C. M.

ISAAC WATTS. 1719.   ARR. from G. F. HANDEL. 1685-1759.

1. Joy to the world; the Lord is come; Let earth re-ceive her King:

Let ev-'ry heart pre-pare Him room, And heav'n and nature sing. And
And heav'n and nature

heav'n and nature sing,   And heav'n, And heav'n and nat-ure sing.
sing,   And heav'n and nature sing.

2 Joy to the earth; the Saviour reigns;
  Let men their songs employ;
  While fields and floods, rocks, hills, and plains,
  Repeat the sounding joy.

3 No more let sins and sorrows grow,
  Nor thorns infest the ground;
  He comes to make His blessings flow
  Far as the curse is found.

4 He rules the world with truth and grace,
  And makes the nations prove
  The glories of His righteousness,
  And wonders of His love.

No. 84. I NEED THEE, LAMB OF GOD.

J. E. RANKIN, D.D.   "Lord, remember me."—LUKE 23: 42.   J. W. SLAUGHENHAUPT.

1. Just as Thou art, by man de-nied, With bleeding hands, and feet, and side,
2. Just as Thou art, unstained by sin, So full of ten-der-ness with-in;
3. Just as Thou art, by God ap-proved, To die for man, di-vine-ly moved,
4. Just as Thou art! so pure, so wise; Complete on earth Thy Sac-ri-fice;

For-sak-en, dy-ing, cru-ci-fied, I need Thee, Lamb of God!
So hu-man all Thy lot hath been; I need Thee, Lamb of God!
To die for man, it Thee be-hooved: I need Thee, Lamb of God!
Tri-umphant now, with-in the skies, I need Thee, Lamb of God!

Chorus.

I need Thee, Lamb of God! I need Thy pre-cious blood:

For-sak-en, dy-ing, cru-ci-fied, I need Thee, Lamb of God!

(83)

No. 85.   I AM FAR FROM THE LAND.

THEODORE. E. PERKINS.

Solo.

1. I am far from the land of my birth, moth-er, I am far from my dwelling and thee,......... But I know thou art kneeling and praying to God, And I feel thou art praying for me.

2. I am lone-ly, and had I but wings, moth-er, I would fly like a bird-ling to thee;......... Yet it's sweet to re-member thy teachings of love, And I feel thou art praying for me.

3. The winds are a-sleep in the caves, moth-er, Our star look-ing down, I can see .... It smiles on me now with its calm mellow light, Ah, yes, thou art praying for me.

Quartette.

There's an ech-o steals o-ver my heart, mother, And floats on the

For the pray'r of the faith-ful is heard, mother, And Je-sus my

And my life will be spared, I am sure, mother, Our Lord will re-

(84)

I AM FAR FROM THE LAND.—Concluded.

deep roll - ing sea, 'Tis the pray'r thou art breath-ing to-
guar- dian will be, He will ans - wer the wish of my
- store me to thee, And we'll thank Him to - geth - er at

night, mother, 'Tis the pray'r thou art breath-ing for me.
soul, mother, The pray'r thou art breath-ing for me.
home, mother, I know thou art pray - ing for me.

Chorus.

I know thou art pray - ing, for me,...... I know thou art

for me,

pray- ing for me......... For I know thou art pray - ing to-

for me,

- night, mother dear, And I know thou art pray-ing for me..........

for me..........

(85)

No. 87. I AM WAITING BY THE RIVER.

WM. O. CUSHING.

DR. THOS. HASTINGS.

1. I am wait-ing by the riv - er, And my heart has wait-ed long;

Now I think I hear the cho - rus Of the an - gel's wel-come song,

Oh, I see the dawn is breaking On the hill-tops of the blest,

"Where the wick - ed cease from troubling, And the wea - ry are at rest."

2 Far away beyond the shadows
 Of this weary vale of tears,
There the tide of bliss is sweeping
 Through the bright and changeless
O! I long to be with Jesus, [years;
 In the mansions of the blest,
"Where the wicked cease from trou-
 bling,
 And the weary are at rest."

3 They are launching on the river,
 From the calm and quiet shore,
And they soon will bear my spirit
 Where the weary sigh no more:
For the tide is swiftly flowing,
 And I long to greet the blest,
"Where the wicked cease from trou-
 bling,
 And the weary are at rest."

LABAN. S. M.

GEO. HEATH, 1781.   Dr. LOWELL MASON, 1830.

1. My soul, be on thy guard, Ten thousand foes a - rise;
2. O watch, and fight, and pray; The bat - tle ne'er give o'er;

The hosts of sin are pressing hard, To draw thee from the skies.
Re - new it bold-ly ev-'ry day, And help di - vine im-plore.

---

90. ARLINGTON. C. M.

Father, I stretch my hands to Thee;
No other help I know :
If Thou withdraw Thyself from me,
Ah, whither shall I go?

2 What did Thine only Son endure
Before I drew my breath!
What pain, what labor, to secure
My soul from endless death!

Author of faith, to Thee I lift
My weary, longing eyes;
Oh, may I now receive that gift;
My soul, without it, dies.

REV. C. WESLEY.

91. HORTON. 7s.

1 Lord, we come before Thee now,
At Thy feet we humbly bow;
Oh, do not our suit disdain ;
Shall we seek Thee, Lord, in vain?

2 In Thine own appointed way
Now we seek Thee; here we stay;

Lord, from hence we would not go,
Till a blessing Thou bestow.

3 Comfort those who weep and mourn;
Let the time of joy return ;
Those that are cast down, lift up ;
Make them strong in faith and hope.

4 Grant that all may seek and find
Thee a God supremely kind :
Heal the sick ; the captive free ;
Let us all rejoice in Thee.

REV. WM. HAMMOND.

92. CHRISTMAS. C. M.

1 Awake, my soul, stretch every nerve,
And press with vigor on ;
A heavenly race demands thy zeal,
And an immortal crown.

2 A cloud of witnesses around,
Hold thee in full survey :
Forget the steps already trod,
And onward urge thy way.

3 'Tis God's all-animating voice
That calls thee from on high :
'Tis His own hand presents the prize
To thine uplifted eye.

REV. PHILIP DODDRIDGE.

No. 93. LO, THE HARVEST IS WHITE.

J. E. RANKIN, D.D.

Rev. S. MORRISON.

1. Reap - ers! O reap - ers! the har - vest is white, And wait-ing the
2. Reap - ers! O reap - ers! the har - vest still waits! And soon will the
3. Reap - ers! O reap - ers! then en - ter the field! And save for the

sick - le to - day: The sha - dows are fall - ing, and
win - ter be - gin; The Hus - band-man asks, what the
Mas - ter His grain: For i - dle - ness sure - ly to

soon comes the night, Bear the sheaves to the gar - ner a - way.
work so be - lates: O then, come, and the sheaves gather in.
you can but yield A sad har - vest of sor - row and pain.

Chorus.

Reap - ers, reap - ers, great your re - ward, When life's la - bors are done:

At the last day, day of the Lord, Shin-ing for aye as the sun.

No. 94. WORK, FOR THE NIGHT IS COMING.

Dr. L. Mason.

1. Work, for the night is com - ing, Work thro' the morn-ing hours,
2. Work, for the night is com - ing, Work thro' the sun - ny noon;
3. Work, for the night is com - ing, Un - der the sun - set skies;

Work while the dew is spark - ling, Work 'mid spring-ing flow'rs;
Fill brightest hours with la - bor, Rest comes sure and soon:
While their bright tints are glow - ing, Work, the day - light flies:

Work when the day grows bright - er, Work in the glow-ing sun;
Give ev - 'ry fly - ing min - ute Something to keep in store;
Work till the last beam fad - eth, Fad - eth to shine no more;

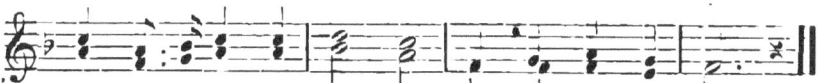

Work, for the night is com - ing, When man's work is done.
Work, for the night is com - ing, When man works no more.
Work while the night is dark - 'ning, When man's work is o'er.

95. NOT HALF HAS EVER BEEN TOLD.

"And the building of the wall of it was jasper; and the city was pure gold,
like unto clear glass."—Rev. 21 : 18.

Rev. A. B. Atchison.   O. F. Presbrey. Arr. J. W. Bischoff.

1. I have read   of   a beau - ti - ful cit - y,   Far a - way in the
2. I have read   of bright mansions in Heav - en, Which the Sav-iour has
3. I have read   of white robes for the right-eous, Of bright crowns which the
4. I have read   of   a Christ so for - giv - ing, That vile sin-ners may

king-dom of   God; I have read how its walls are of jas - per, How its
gone to   pre - pare; Where the saints who on earth have been faithful, Rest for-
glo - ri - fied wear, When our Fa-ther shall bid them "Come en- ter, And my
ask   and   re - ceive Peace and par-don from ev - 'ry transgres-sion, If when

streets are all gold-en and   broad. In the midst of   the street is life's
ev - er with Christ o - ver there; There no sin   ev - er en - ters, nor
glo - ry   e - ter - nal - ly   share;" How the right-eous are   ev - er more
ask - ing they on - ly   be - lieve.   I have read how He'll guide and pro-

By permission.   (90)

No. 99. SOUND THE BATTLE CRY.

W. F. S. 1869.

WM. F. SHERWIN.

Vigorously, in march time.

1. Sound the bat - tle cry, See! the foe is nigh; Raise the standard high
2. Strong to meet the foe, Marching on we go, While our cause we know
3. Oh! thou God of all, Hear us when we call, Help us one and all.

For the Lord; Gird your ar - mor on, Stand firm ev - ery one,
Must pre - vail; Shield and ban - ner bright Gleaming in the light,
By Thy grace; When the bat - tle's done, And the vic - t'ry won,

No. 100. THE CLEANSING WAVE.

Mrs. Phœbe Palmer.   Mrs. Jos. F. Knapp.

1. Oh, now I see the crimson wave, The fountain deep and wide;
2. I rise to walk in heaven's own light A-bove the world and sin,
3. A-maz ing grace! 'tis heaven be-low To feel the blood ap-plied;

Je - sus, my Lord, might - y to save, Points to His wounded side,
With heart made pure, and garments white, And Christ enthroned with - in.
And Je - sus, on - ly Je - sus know, My Je - sus cru - ci - fied.

Chorus.

The cleansing stream I see! I see! I plunge, and oh, it cleanseth me,

Oh, praise the Lord, it cleanseth me! It cleanseth me, yes, cleanseth me.

By permission.   (96)

No. 101. WONDERFUL GRACE.

Rev. W. H. Burrell. " By grace ye are saved."—Eph. 2 : 5. Rev. I. Baltzell.

1. 'Tis grace! 'tis grace! 'tis wonder - ful grace! This great sal-va - tion brings;
2. 'Tis grace! 'tis grace! 'tis wonder - ful grace! Which saves the soul from sin:

The soul, de - liv - ered of its load In sweet - est rap - ture sings.
The power of ris - ing e - vil slays, And reigns supreme with - in.

Chorus.

'Tis grace!...... 'Tis grace!...... Won-der - ful, won-der - ful

'Tis won-der-ful grace ! 'Tis wonder - ful grace !

grace!.......... 'Tis grace!...... 'Tis grace!...........

won - der - ful grace! 'Tis won - der - ful grace! 'Tis won - der - ful grace !

Flowing still freely for me.

3.

'Tis grace! 'tis grace! 'tis wonderful grace !
Its streams are full and free;
Are flowing now for all the race;
They even flow to me.

(97)

No. 102. SWEET CANAAN LAND.

J. E. RANKIN, D.D. "A land flowing with milk and honey."—JOSH. 5 : 6.   J. E. RANKIN.

1. Heav'n is to me no for-eign strand, No for-eign strand to me; It
2. Heav'n is to me sweet Canaan land, Sweet Canaan land to me! Its
3. With milk and ho - ney flows that land, Sweet Canaan land to me! With
4. Come with me to this Canaan land, Sweet Canaan land to thee! Why

is my heart's sweet Canaan land, It is my home to be; It
mansions fair I see them stand, I see them stand for me; For
ver - dure fair its fields expand: Sweet Canaan land to me! My
on its bor - ders wait - ing stand? Thy rest, too, it may be: Come

is the rest for which I long: It is the theme of all my song.
there before His Father's face, Je - sus for me prepares a place.
wand'rings and my sins all o'er: My soul's sweet rest for - ev - er-more.
with me, walk its fields so fair, Come, with me all its glo - ries share.

Refrain.

Sweet Canaan land! Sweet Canaan land! Thy fields of green I see; Sweet

SWEET CANAAN LAND.—Concluded.

Canaan land! Sweet Canaan land! What can di-vide from thee?

---

103. QUEBEC. L. M.

1 Sun of my soul, Thou Saviour dear!
It is not night if Thou be near;
Oh, may no earth-born cloud arise
To hide Thee from Thy servant's eyes.

2 When soft the dews of kindly sleep
My wearied eyelids gently steep,
Be my last thought, how sweet to rest
Forever on my Saviour's breast!

3 Abide with me from morn till eve,
For without Thee I cannot live;
Abide with me when night is nigh,
For without Thee I dare not die.

4 Come near to bless us when we wake,
Ere through the world our way we
take,
Till in the ocean of Thy love
We lose ourselves in heaven above.

WATTS.

104. DENNIS. S. M.

1 Blest be the tie that binds
Our hearts in Christian love;
The fellowship of kindred minds
Is like to that above.

2 Before our Father's throne
We pour our ardent prayers;
Our fears, our hopes, our aims are one,
Our comforts and our cares.

3 We share our mutual woes,
Our mutual burdens bear;
And often for each other flows
The sympathizing tear.

REV. JOHN FAWCETT.

105. COME, YE DISCONSOLATE.
11s & 10s.

1 Come, ye disconsolate, where'er ye lan-
guish,
Come to the mercy-seat, fervently
kneel;
Here bring your wounded hearts, here
tell your anguish, [not heal.
Earth has no sorrow that heaven can-

2 Joy of the desolate, light of the straying,
Hope of the penitent, fadeless and
pure, [ing,
Here speaks the Comforter, tenderly say-
Earth has no sorrow that heaven can-
not cure.

3 Here see the bread of life; see waters
flowing [from above;
Forth from the throne of God, pure
Come to the feast of love; come ever
knowing
Earth has no sorrow but heaven can
remove.

106. SERENITY. C. M.

1 The twilight falls, the night is near,
I fold my work away,
And kneel to One who bends to hear
The story of the day.

2 The old, old story; yet I kneel
To tell it at Thy call;
And cares grow lighter as I feel
That Jesus knows them all.

3 Thou knowest all; I lean my head,
My weary eyelids close;
Content and glad awhile to tread
This path, since Jesus knows.

(99)

1 How firm a foundation, ye saints of the Lord,
  Is laid for your faith in His excellent word!
  What more can He say than to you He hath said—
  You, who unto Jesus for refuge have fled?

2 Fear not; I am with thee; O, be not dismayed:
  I, I am thy God, and will still give thee aid;
  I'll strengthen thee, help thee, and cause thee to stand,
  Upheld by my righteous omnipotent hand.

3 When through the deep waters I call thee to go,
  The rivers of woe shall not thee overflow:
  For I will be with thee, thy troubles to bless,
  And sanctify to thee thy deepest distress.

4 When through fiery trials thy pathway shall lie,
  My grace, all-sufficient, shall be thy supply;
  The flame shall not hurt thee; I only design
  Thy dross to consume, and thy gold to refine.

5 E'en down to old age, all my people shall prove
  My sovereign, eternal, unchangeable love;
  And when hoary hairs shall their temples adorn,
  Like lambs they shall still in my bosom be borne.

6 The soul that on Jesus hath leaned for repose,
  I will not, I will not desert to his foes:
  That soul, though all hell should endeavor to shake,
  I'll never, no, never, no, never forsake.

REV. JOHN KIRKHAM.

TRUST, OH TRUST YOUR FATHER.

"Consider the lilies, how they grow."—Matt. 6 : 28.

J. E. RANKIN, D.D.   SILCHER.

1. Lo, the li - lies, how they grow, 'Neath Spring rains de-scend-ing;
2. Take no tho't what ye shall eat, Trou - ble do not bor-row;
3. Trust, oh, trust your Fa-ther's care, Liv - ing Bread He's giv - en;

'Tis your Fa - ther clothes them so, Their sweet gra - ces blend-ing:
He who gives all crea-tures meat, Will pro - vide to - mor-row:
Rai - ment, too, both white and fair, He pro - vides in heav - en:

Why, then, are ye full of care, Since His love is eve - ry-where?
He who hears the ra - ven's cry, Sure - ly can - not you de - ny,
He will there His work com-plete, For the life is more than meat,

Trust, oh, trust your Fa - ther. Trust, oh, trust your Fa - ther.
Trust, oh, trust your Fa - ther. Trust, oh, trust your Fa - ther.
Trust, oh, trust your Fa - ther, Trust, oh, trust your Fa - ther.

No. 109.   GLOOMY, STILL GLOOMY.

CHARLES F. DEEMS.   (*Storm Hymn.*)

1. Gloom - y, still gloom - y, the rain - drops are fall - ing,
2. God of cre - a - tion, when storm-clouds are rag - ing,

Voic - es from out the thick dark - ness are call - ing;
Thund'rings and light - nings in bat - tle en - gag - ing,

Light-nings are toss - ing their torch - es on high, And gleam o'er the
Shield Thou our hearts by the wings of Thy love, While gloom mantles

bat - tle - ment clouds of the sky, While the crash of the
round us, and strife raves a - bove! While our life's lat - est

thun - der doth sol - emn- ly roll, Ac - cents that deep - en the
tem - pest has hushed its a - larms, Gent - ly our spir - it up-

awe of the soul. Fa - ther, de - fend us! Fa - ther, for-give us!
bear in Thine arms. Fa - ther, de - fend us! Fa - ther, for-give us!

Fa - ther, re - ceive us, Thro' Je - sus Christ our Lord! A - MEN.

No. 110. EVENING HYMN.

1 Fading, still fading, the last beam is shining,
  Father in heaven, the day is declining,
  Safety and innocence fly with the light,
  Temptation and danger walk forth with the night;
  From the fall of the shade till the morning bells chime,
  Shield us from danger, save us from crime.
    Father, have mercy, Father, have mercy,
  Father, have mercy through Jesus Christ our Lord.

2 Father in heaven! O hear when we call;
  Hear for Christ's sake, who is Saviour of all;
  Feeble and fainting we trust in Thy might,
  In doubting and darkness Thy love be our light.
  Let us sleep on Thy breast while the night taper burns,
  Wake in Thy arms when morning returns.
    Father, have mercy, Father, have mercy,
  Father, have mercy through Jesus Christ our Lord. AMEN.

No. 112. REFUGE.

"God is a refuge for us."—Psalms, 62: 8

JOSEPHINE POLLARD. J. W. BISCHOFF.

Tenderly.

1. In the dark-est hour That my heart may know,
2. Here there is no ref-uge For the soul op-pressed;
3. Poor and weak and wretched, Full of fears and woe,
4. Bound in cords of an-guish, By my sins dis-mayed;
5. Joy in trib-u-la-tion! Hope that sets me free!

Out of Sa-tan's pow-er. Whith-er shall I go?
Whith-er shall I journey? Whith-er seek for rest?
To be free from torment, Whith-er can I go?
Whith-er, then, ah, whith-er, Can I look for aid?
Je-sus, my sal-va-tion, Lo! I turn to Thee.

Chorus. Cheerfully.

To Je-sus! To Je-sus! On-ly un-to Je-sus, The

Sav-iour so com-pas-sion-ate, The sin-ner's on-ly Friend. The

Saviour so com-pas-sion-ate, The sin-ner's on-ly Friend.

By permission. (104)

No. 113. MAKE ROOM FOR JESUS.

"There was no room for them at the inn."—LUKE 2 : 7.

REV. ALEXANDER CLARK, D.D.   WM. G. FISCHER.

1. Make room for Je - sus! room! room! sad heart, Be-guiled and sick of sin;
2. Make room for Je - sus! room! make room! His hand is at the door:
3. Make room for Je - sus! soul of mine. He waits re-sponse to - day;
3. Make room for Je - sus! by - and - by, 'Midst saint and ser - a - phim,

Bid eve - ry al - ien guest de - part, And rise and let Him in.
He comes to ban - ish guilt and gloom, And bless thee more and more.
His smile is peace, His grace di - vine, Oh, turn Him not a - way.
He'll wel-come to His throne on high The soul that wel-comed Him.

Chorus.

Make room, sad heart, make room, make room, Bid al - ien guests de - part,

Oh, let the Mas - ter in, sad heart: A - rise, make room, make room!

By permission.   (105)

No. 114.   NOTHING BUT LEAVES!

Mrs. Lucy E. Akerman.

S. J. Vail, by per.

1. Noth-ing but leaves! The Spir-it grieves O'er years of wast-ed
2. Noth-ing but leaves! No gath-er'd sheaves Of life's fair rip-'ning

life; O'er sins in-dulged while con-science slept, O'er
grain: We sow our seeds; lo! tares and weeds—Words,

vows and prom-is-es un-kept, And reap from years of
i-dle words, for earn-est deeds, Then reap, with toil and

strife— Nothing but leaves! Nothing but leaves!
pain, Nothing but leaves! Nothing but leaves!

3 Nothing but leaves! sad mem'ry
No veil to hide the past: [weaves
And as we trace our weary way,
And count each lost and misspent
We sadly find at last— [day,
Nothing but leaves! nothing but
leaves!

4 Ah, who shall thus the Master meet,
And bring but withered leaves?
Ah, who shall at the Saviour's feet,
Before the awful judgment-seat,
Lay down for golden sheaves,
Nothing but leaves! nothing but
leaves!

No. 115. SAVE THE BOY!

Mrs. S. C. Ellsworth.　　　　　　　　　　　　　　　　　W. W. Bentley.

Solo.

1. Once he was so light and fair, Glad and light and free, Fill'd my soul with
2. Once he was so brave and true, Shunn'd the tempter's pow'r, Once for right he

peace and joy, Life was dear to me; But he took the fa - tal glass,
firm- ly stood, Till that dreadful hour; Bright and sparkling was the cup,

'Twas a fleet-ing joy, Drank, and lo, the hand of death Grasp'd my darling boy.
Seem'd without al-loy, Fair the band that captive led My poor wand'ring boy.

Chorus.

Save the boy! Save the boy! Heav'n will ring with joy;

Lov - ing hearts are plead - ing now, Save, O save the boy!

3 Once he was my only hope,
　Source of joy and pride,
Then I thought that love might clasp,
　Hold him to my side;
But to-day my boy forsakes
　Home with all its joy,
Far in sin he's wand'ring now:
　Save, oh, save my boy!—Cho.

4 Tell him though he's wandered far
　Love can never die,
Lives in hope of his return,
　Looks with patient eye;
Loving hearts have pleaded long,
　Pray'd for light and joy,
Keeping still a welcome there
　For the wandering boy.—Cho.

(107)

No. 116. ONWARD, CHRISTIAN SOLDIERS.

Rev. S. B. Gould.   Joseph Haydn. Arr.

1. Onward, Christian soldiers, Marching as to war, With the Cross of Je- sus
2. Like a mighty ar-my Moves the Church of God; Brothers, we are treading

Go-ing on be - fore, Christ the Royal Mas- ter   Leads against the foe,
Where the saints have trod; We are not di- vid- ed,   All one bod-y   we;

Chorus.

Forward in-to   bat - tle, See his banners   go. ⎫ Onward, Christian soldiers,
One in hope and doc-trine, One in char-i - ty. ⎭

Marching as to   war, With the Cross of Je - sus   Go-ing on be - fore.

3 Crowns and thrones may perish,
　Kingdoms rise and wane,
　But the Church of Jesus
　Constant will remain ;
　Gates of hell can never
　'Gainst that Church prevail ;
　We have Christ's own promise,
　And that cannot fail.

4 Onward, then, ye people,
　Join our happy throng,
　Blend with ours your voices
　In the triumph song ;
　Glory, laud, and honor,
　Unto Christ the King,
　This through countless ages
　Men and angels sing.

ITALIAN HYMN.

F. GIARDINI.

No. 138.

1 Come, Thou Almighty King,
Help us Thy name to sing,
Help us to praise;
Father, all-glorious,
O'er all victorious,
Come, and reign over us,
Ancient of Days.

2 Jesus, our Lord, descend;
From all our foes defend,
Nor let us fall;
Let Thine almighty aid
Our sure defence be made,
Our souls on Thee be stayed;
Lord, hear our call.

3 Come, Thou Incarnate Word,
Gird on Thy mighty sword;
Our prayer attend;
Come, and Thy people bless;
Come, give Thy word success;
Spirit of holiness,
On us descend.

4 Come, Holy Comforter,
Thy sacred witness bear,
In this glad hour;
Thou, who almighty art,
Now rule in every heart,
And ne'er from us depart,
Spirit of power.

5 To Thee, great One in Three,   –
The highest praises be,
Hence evermore;
Thy sovereign majesty
May we in glory see.
And to eternity
Love and adore.

No. 139.

1 Glory to God on high!
Let heaven and earth reply,
"Praise ye His name!"
Angels, His love adore,
Who all our sorrows bore;
Saints, sing for ever more,
"Worthy the Lamb."

2 Ye, who surround the throne,
Cheerfully join in one,
Praising His name:
Ye, who have felt His blood
Sealing your peace with God,
Sound through the earth abroad,
"Worthy the Lamb!"

3 Join all the ransomed race,
Our Lord and God to bless:
Praise ye His name.
In Him we will rejoice,
Making a cheerful noise,
Shouting with heart and voice,
"Worthy the Lamb!"

4 Soon must we change our place,
Yet will we never cease
Praising His name:
Still will we tribute bring;
Hail Him our gracious King;
And through all ages sing,
"Worthy the Lamb!"

No. 140.

1 Thee, Lord our God alone,
The high and holy One,
Our hearts adore;
Now to the Father raise,
And to the Son, our praise,
And to the Spirit's grace,
Hence, evermore.

No. 117. THE ROCK THAT IS HIGHER.

E. JOHNSON.

WM. G. FISCHER, by per.

1. Oh, sometimes the shadows are deep, And rough seems the path to the goal,
2. Oh, sometimes how long seems the day, And sometimes how weary my feet;
3. Oh, near to the Rock let me keep, If blessings, or sorrows prevail;

And sorrows sometimes how they sweep, Like tempests down over the soul.
But toil-ing in life's dusty way, The Rock's blessed shadow how sweet.
Or climbing the mountain way steep, Or walking the shad-ow-y vale.

Chorus.

Oh, then to the Rock let me fly, (let me fly,) To the Rock that is high-er than I: is high-er than I:

Oh, then to the Rock let me fly, (let me fly,) To the Rock that is high-er than I.

No. 118. THE WATERS ARE TROUBLED.

"The angel troubled the water."—JOHN 5 : 4.

J. E. RANKIN, D D.

Rev. S. MORRISON.

1. The wa-ters are troubled, The an - gel is here; The fountain of
2. The wa-ters are troubled, No long-er de - lay; The fountain of

mercy Flows heal-ing and clear; O come in your sorrow, And
mercy Has heal-ing to - day; Then why will you linger? Since

Slow.

come in your sin; The wa-ters are troubled: Step in, O step in.
life you may win; The wa-ters are troubled: Step in, O step in.

3 The waters are troubled!
   The first will be healed;
   The fountain of mercy,
   Alas! may be sealed:
   Another, before you,
   Salvation may win:
   The waters are troubled!
   Step in, O step in!

4 The waters are troubled!
   The angel still waits;
   He pauses in peril
   Who halts and debates:
   Give over your falt'ring—
   Your struggles within:
   The waters are troubled!
   Step in, O step in!

No. 119. A SINNER FORGIVEN.

"He said unto her, thy sins are forgiven."—LUKE 7 : 48.

ENGLISH.   Arranged.

1. To the hall of the feast came the sin - ful and fair; She heard in the
2. The frown and the murmur went round thro' them all. That one so un -
3. She heard but the Sa-viour: she spoke but with sighs: She dare not look
4. In the sky, af - ter tem - pest, as shin-eth the bow. — In the glance of the

cit - y that Je - sus was there; Un - heed-ing the splen-dor that
hallowed should tread in that hall; And some said the poor would be
up to the heaven of His eyes; And the hot tears gush'd forth at each
sunbeam, as melt-eth the snow, He looked on that lost one: her

blazed on the board. She si - lent - ly knelt at the feet of the
ob - jects more meet. As the wealth of her per - fume she shower'd on His
heave of her breast. As her lips to His san - dals were throbbing - ly
sins were forgiven, And the sin - ner went forth in the beau - ty of

Lord, She si - lent - ly knelt at the feet of the Lord.
feet, As the wealth of her per - fume she shower'd on His feet.
pressed, As her lips to His san - dals were throbbing - ly pressed.
heaven, And the sin - ner went forth in the beau - ty of heaven.

HOME, SWEET HOME.

JOHN HOWARD PAYNE.   Sicilian Air. Sir HENRY R. BISHOP.

Andante.

1. 'Mid pleasures and pal - a - ces tho' we may roam, Be it ev - er so
2. An ex - ile from home splendor daz- zles in vain ; Oh, give me my

hum- ble, there's no place like home. A charm from the skies seems to
low - ly thatch'd cot- tage a - gain, The birds sing-ing gai - ly, that

hal-low us there, Which, seek thro' the world, is ne'er met with elsewhere.
come at my call ; Give me these, with the peace of mind, dearer than all.

Home, home, sweet, sweet home ! There's no   place like home, There's no   place like home.
Home, home, etc.

3 How sweet 'tis to sit 'neath a fond father's smile,
  And the cares of a mother to soothe and beguile;
  Let others delight 'mid new pleasures to roam,
  But give me, oh! give me the pleasures of home.
        Home! home! sweet, sweet home!
  But give me, oh! give me the pleasures of home.

4 To thee I'll return, over-burdened with care,
  The heart's dearest solace will smile on me there;
  No more from that cottage again will I roam,
  Be it ever so humble, there's no place like home.
        Home! home! sweet, sweet home!
  There's no place like home ; there's no place like home.

No. 121. YET THERE IS ROOM.

Rev. H. Bonar. "Yet there is room."—Luke 14 : 22. Ira D. Sankey.

Slow, with expression.

1. Yet there is room! The Lamb's bright hall of song,
With its fair glo - ry, beck - ons thee a - long;
Room, room, still room! Oh, en - ter, en - ter now!

2 Day is declining, and the sun is low:
The shadows lengthen, light makes haste to go:
Room, room, still room! oh, enter, enter now!

3 The bridal hall is filling for the feast:
Pass in, pass in, and be the Bridegroom's guest:
Room, room, still room! oh, enter, enter now!

4 It fills, it fills, that hall of jubilee!
Make haste, make haste; 'tis not too full for thee:
Room, room, still room! oh, enter, enter now!

5 Yet there is room! Still open stands the gate,
The gate of love; it is not yet too late:
Room, room, still room! oh, enter, enter now;

6 Pass in, pass in! That banquet is for thee;
That cup of everlasting love is free:
Room, room, still room! oh, enter, enter now!

7 All heaven is there, all joy! Go in, go in;
The angels beckon thee the prize to win:
Room, room, still room! oh, enter, enter now!

8 Louder and sweeter sounds the loving call:
Come lingerer, come; enter that festal hall:
Room, room, still room! oh, enter, enter now!

9 Ere night that gate may close, and seal thy doom:
Then the last, low, long cry:—"No room, no room!"
No room, no room:—oh, woful cry, "No room!"

By permission. (114)

No. 122. SCATTER SEEDS OF KINDNESS.

Mrs. E. H. Gates.

S. J. Vail. Cop. 1870.

1. Let us gath-er up the sunbeams Ly-ing all a-round our path;
2. Strange, we nev-er prize the mu-sic Till the sweet-voiced bird has flown!
3. If we knew the ba-by fin-gers, Press'd a-gainst the win-dow pane,
4. Ah! those lit-tle ice-cold fin-gers, How they point our mem'ries back

Let us keep the wheat and ro-ses, Cast-ing out the thorns and chaff;
Strange, that we should slight the violets, Till the love-ly flow'rs are gone!
Would be cold and stiff to-morrow—Nev-er troub-le us a-gain—
To the has-ty words and actions Strewn a-long our back-ward track!

Let us find our sweet-est com-fort In the bless-ings of to-day,
Strange, that summer skies and sunshine Nev-er seem one half so fair,
Would the bright eyes of our dar-ling Catch the frown up-on our brow!
How those lit-tle hands re-mind us, As in snow-y grace they lie,

With a pa-tient hand re-moving All the bri-ers from the way.
As when winter's snow-y pinions Shake the white down in the air.
Would the print of ro-sy fin-gers Vex us then as they do now?
Not to scat-ter thorns—but ro-ses— For our reap-ing by and by.

IN SIGHT OF THE CRYSTAL SEA.

"Son, remember."—LUKE 15 : 25.

J. E. RANKIN, D.D.

J. W. BISCHOFF.

Rather slow.

1. I sat a - lone with life's mem -o - ries In sight of the crys-tal sea;
2. I thought me then of my childhood days, The prayer at my mother's knee

And I saw the thrones of the star-crown'd ones, With never a crown for me.
Of the counsels grave that my father gave—The wrath I was warned to flee

And then the voice of the Judge said, "Come," Of the Judge on the great white thron
I said, "Is it then to late, too late? Shut without. must I stand for aye?

And I saw the star-crowned take their seats, But none could I call my own.
And the Judge, will He say, "I know you not," How-e'er I may knock and pra

3.

I thought, I thought of the days of God
  I'd wasted in folly and sin— [knock'd,
Of the times I'd mock'd when the Saviour
  And I would not let Him in.
I thought, I thought of the vows I'd made
  When I lay at death's dark door—
"Would He spare my life, I'd give up the
    strife,
  And serve Him forever more."

4.

I heard a voice, like the voice of God—
  "Remember, remember, my son!
Remember thy ways in the former days,
  The crowns that thou might'st have
    won!"   [on,
I thought, I thought and my thoughts ran
  Like the tide of a sunless sea—
"Am I living or dead?" to myself I said,
  "An end is there ne'er to be?"

5.

It seemed as though I woke from a dream,
  How sweet was the light of day!
Melodious sounded the Sabbath bells
  From towers that were far away.
I then became as a little child,
  And I wept, and wept afresh;
For the Lord had taken my heart of stone,
  And given a heart of flesh.

6.

Still oft I sit with life's memories,
  And think of the crystal sea; [ones;
And I see the thrones of the star-crowned
  I know there's a crown for me.
And when the voice of the Judge says
  "Come,"
Of the Judge on the great white throne
I know mid the thrones of the star-crown-
  ed ones
There's one I shall call my own.

No. 124.   COME TO JESUS.

1 Come to Jesus, come to Jesus,
    Come to Jesus just now.
  Just now come to Jesus,
    Come to Jesus just now;
2 He will save you, etc.
3 He is able, etc.
4 He is willing, etc.

5 He is waiting, etc.
6 He will hear you, etc.
7 He will cleanse you, etc.
8 He'll renew you, etc.
9 He'll forgive you, etc.
10 If you trust Him, etc.
11 He will save you, etc.

No. 125.   I LOVE TO STEAL AWHILE AWAY.

1 I love to steal awhile away
    From every cumbering care,
  And spend the hours of setting day
    In humble, grateful prayer.

2 I love in solitude to shed
    The penitential tear,
  And all His promises to plead
    Where none but God can hear.

3 I love to think on mercies past,
    And future good implore,
  And all my cares and sorrows cast
    On Him whom I adore.

4 I love by faith to take a view
    Of brighter scenes in heaven;
  The prospect doth my strength renew,
    While here by temptests driven.
                    MRS. PHEBE H. BROWN.

No. 126.   SWEET HOUR OF PRAYER.

1 Sweet hour of prayer! sweet hour of
    prayer!
  That calls me from a world of care,
  And bids me at my Father's throne
  Make all my wants and wishes known;
  In seasons of distress and grief
  My soul has often found relief,
  And oft escaped the tempter's snare
  By thy return, sweet hour of prayer.

2 Sweet hour of prayer! sweet hour of
    prayer!
  Thy wings shall my petition bear
  To Him whose truth and faithfulness
  Engage the waiting soul to bless;
  And since He bids me seek His face,
  Believe His word and trust His grace,
  I'll cast on him my every care,
  And wait for thee, sweet hour of prayer.

No. 127. WHERE DO YOU JOURNEY?

Mrs. MARY A. KIDDER.

S. J. VAIL.

Solo.

1. Oh! where do you journey, my brother, Oh! where do you journey, I pray?
2. Oh! what is your mission, my brother, Oh! what is your mission be-low?
3. Oh! yes you will meet us, my brother, God keep us from weakness and sin;

And where do you journey, my sis-ter? For stormy and dark is the way;
And what is your mission, my sis-ter, As jour-ney-ing onward we go?
And bear-ing the cross, we, my sis-ter, The crown will endeavor to win;

Duet.

We're journeying onward to Ca-naan, Thro' suff'ring and tri-al and care;
Our mis-sion is prac-ticing mer-cy, Sweet char-i-ty, patience, and love,
We'll walk thro' the vale and the shadow, Thro' suff'ring, and tri-al, and care;

And when we get safe-ly to glo-ry, Oh! say, shall we meet you all there?
And foll'wing the footsteps of Je-sus That lead to the mansions a-bove.
And when you get safe-ly to glo-ry, You'll meet, yes, you'll meet us all there.

Chorus.

Oh! say, shall we meet you all there? Oh! say, shall we meet you all there?

And when we get safe-ly to glo-ry, Oh! say shall we meet you all there?

By permission.

No. 128. ARISE, MY SOUL, ARISE.

Rev. Charles Wesley

J. Edson.

1. A - rise my soul, a - rise, Shake off thy guil - ty fears,
The bleed- ing sac - ri - fice In my be - half ap - pears;
Be - fore the throne my Sure - ty stands, My name is writ - ten
on His hands, My name is writ - ten on His hands.

2 He ever lives above,
   For me to intercede,
His all redeeming love,
   His precious blood to plead;
His blood atoned for all our race,
And sprinkles now the throne of grace.

3 Five bleeding wounds He bears,
   Received on Calvary;
They pour effectual prayers,
   They strongly plead for me:
Forgive him, oh, forgive, they cry,
Nor let that ransomed sinner die.

4 The Father hears him pray,
   His dear anointed One:
He cannot turn away
   The presence of his Son:
His Spirit answers to the blood,
And tells me I am born of God.

5 My God is reconciled;
   His pardoning voice I hear;
He owns me for His child;
   I can no longer fear;
With confidence I now draw nigh,
And Father, Abba, Father, cry.

(119)

COMING BY AND BY.

"It shall come to pass in the last days."—Isa. ii: 2.

R. L.   R. LOWRY.

1. A bet-ter day is com-ing, A morning promised long, When gird-ed
2. The boast of haughty er-ror No more will fill the air; But age and
3. O for that ho-ly dawn-ing, We watch, and wait, and pray, Till o'er the

right with ho-ly might Will o-ver-throw the wrong; When God the Lord will
youth will love the truth, And spread it ev-'ry-where. No more from want and
height the morning light Shall drive the gloom a-way; And when the heav'n-ly

list-en To ev-'ry plaintive sigh, And stretch His hands o'er ev-'ry land
sor-row, Will come the hopeless cry; And strife will cease, and perfect peace
glo-ry Shall flood the earth and sky, We'll bless the Lord for all His word,

Refrain.

With jus-tice by and by.
Will flourish by and by. } Com-ing by and by, coming by and by,
And praise Him by and by.

The bet-ter day is coming, The morning draweth nigh; Coming by and by,

coming by and by! The welcome dawn will hasten on, 'Tis coming by and by.

No. 130. WHITER, THAN SNOW.

JAMES NICHOLSON.

WM. G. FISCHER, by per.

1. Dear Je - sus, I long to be per- fect - ly whole, I want Thee for -
2. Dear Je - sus, come down from Thy throne in the skies, And help me to

- ev - er to live in my soul; Break down ev - 'ry i - dol, cast
make a complete sac - ri - fice; I give up my - self, and what-

out ev-'ry foe; Now wash me, and I shall be whit - er than snow.
- ev - er I know: Now wash me, and I shall be whit - er than snow.

Chorus.

Whit - er than snow, yes, whit- er than snow; Now wash me, and

I shall be whit- er than snow.

3.
Dear Jesus, for this I most humbly
entreat;
I wait, blessed Lord, sitting low at
Thy feet.
By faith, for my cleansing, I see the
blood flow—
Now wash me, and I shall be whiter
than snow.

SELECTED HYMNS.

131. BOYLSTON. S. M.

1 Jesus, who knows full well
  The heart of every saint,
Invites us all our griefs to tell,
  To pray, and never faint.

2 He bows His gracious ear—
  We never plead in vain;
Then let us wait till He appear,
  And pray, and pray again.

3 Though unbelief suggest
  "Why should we longer wait?"
He bids us never give Him rest,
  But knock at mercy's gate.

4 Then let us earnest cry,
  And never faint in prayer;
He sees, He hears, and from on high
  Will make our cause His care.
         JOHN NEWTON.

132. DUKE STREET. L. M.

1 Stand up, my soul, shake off thy fears,
  And gird the gospel armor on;
March to the gates of endless joy,
  Where Jesus, thy great Captain's gone.

2 Hell and thy sins resist thy course,
  But hell and sin are vanquished foes;
Thy Jesus nailed them to the cross
  And sung the triumph when He rose.

3 Then let my soul march boldly on,
  Press forward to the heavenly gate;
There peace and joy eternal reign,
  And glittering robes for conquerors wait.

4 There shall I wear a starry crown,
  And triumph in immortal grace;
While all the armies of the skies
  Join in my glorious Leader's praise.
         ISAAC WATTS.

133. WEBB. 7s & 6s.

1 When shall the voice of singing
  Flow joyfully along.
When hill and valley ringing
  With one triumphant song,
Proclaim the contest ended.
  And Him who once was slain,
Again to earth descended.
  In righteousness to reign?

---

2 Then from the lofty mountains
  The sacred shout shall fly;
And shady vales and fountains
  Shall echo the reply;
High tower and lowly dwelling
  Shall send the chorus round;
All "Hallelujah" swelling
  In one eternal sound.
      JAMES EDMESTON, 1822.

134. SICILY. 8s & 7s.

1 Lord dismiss us with thy blessing,
  Fill our hearts with joy and peace;
Let us each, Thy love possessing,
  Triumph in redeeming grace.
Oh, refresh us, oh, refresh us,
  Trav'ling through this wilderness.

2 Thanks we give, and adoration,
  For Thy gospel's joyful sound;
May the fruits of thy salvation
  In our hearts and lives abound;
May Thy presence, may Thy presence
  With us evermore be found.

135. WEBB. 7s & 6s.

1 Stand up! stand up for Jesus!
  Ye soldiers of the cross;
Lift high His royal banner,
  It must not suffer loss;
From victory unto victory
  His army He shall lead,
Till every foe is vanquished,
  And Christ is Lord indeed.

2 Stand up! stand up for Jesus!
  Stand in His strength alone;
The arm of flesh will fail you—
  Ye dare not trust your own;
Put on the gospel armor,
  And, watching unto prayer,
Where duty calls, or danger,
  Be never wanting there.

3 Stand up! stand up for Jesus!
  The strife will not be long;
This day the noise of battle,
  The next the victor's song.
To him that overcometh
  A crown of life shall be;
He with the King of Glory
  Shall reign eternally.

    BALERMA. C. M.

To Father, Son, and Holy Ghost,
  One God, whom we adore,
Be glory as it was, is now,
  And shall be evermore.

136. LENOX. H. M.

1 Blow ye the trumpet, blow
  The gladly solemn sound;
  Let all the nations know,
  To earth's remotest bound,
  The year of Jubilee is come;
  Return, ye ransomed sinners, home.

2 Jesus, our great High Priest,
  Has full atonement made;
  Ye weary spirits rest;
  Ye mourning souls be glad;
  The year of Jubilee is come;
  Return, ye ransomed sinners, home.

3 Exalt the Lamb of God,
  The sin-atoning Lamb;
  Redemption by his blood
  Through all the world proclaim;
  The year of Jubilee is come;
  Return, ye ransomed sinners, home.

137. LENOX. H. M.

1 Ye tribes of Adam, join
  With heaven, and earth, and seas,
  And offer notes divine
  To your Creator's praise:
  Ye holy throng of angels bright,
  In worlds of light, begin the song.

2 Thou sun, with dazzling rays,
  And moon, that rul'st the night,
  Shine to your Maker's praise,
  With stars of twinkling light:
  His power declare, ye floods on high,
  And clouds that fly in empty air.

3 The shining worlds above
  In glorious order stand;
  Or in swift courses move
  By His supreme command:
  He spake the word, and all their frame
  From nothing came, to praise the Lord.

4 Ye vapors, hail, and snow,
  Praise ye th' almighty Lord;
  And stormy winds that blow
  To execute His word: [roar,
  When lightnings shine, or thunders
  Let earth adore His hand divine.

138. WILL YOU GO?

1 We're trav'ling home to heaven above;
  ‖: Will you go? :‖
  To sing the Saviour's dying love;
  ‖: Will you go? :‖
  Millions have reached that blest abode,
  Anointed kings and priests to God;
  And millions more are on the road;
  ‖: Will you go? :‖

2 We're going to walk the plains of light;
  ‖: Will you go? :‖
  Far, far from curse and death and night;
  ‖: Will you go? :‖

The crown of life we then shall wear,
  The conqueror's palm we then shall bear,
  And all the joys of heaven we'll share;
  ‖: Will you go? :‖

3 The way to heaven is straight and plain,
  ‖: Will you go? :‖
  Repent, believe, be born again;
  ‖: Will you go? :‖
  The Saviour cries aloud to thee,
  "Take up your cross and follow me,
  And thou shalt my salvation see;"
  ‖: Will you go? :‖

139. BOYLSTON. S. M.

1 And can I yet delay
  My little all to give?
  To tear from earth my soul away
  For Jesus to receive?

2 Nay, but I yield, I yield;
  I can hold out no more;
  I sink, by dying love compelled,
  And own Thee conqueror.

3 Though late, I all forsake;
  My friends, my all, resign;
  Gracious Redeemer, take, O take
  And seal me ever Thine.

4 Come, and possess me whole,
  Nor hence again remove;
  Settle and fix my wav'ring soul
  With all Thy weight of love.
            REV. CHAS. WESLEY.

140. BOYLSTON. S. M.

1 The Lord my Shepherd is,
  I shall be well supplied;
  Since He is mine, and I am His,
  What can I want beside?

2 He leads me to the place
  Where heavenly pasture grows;
  Where living waters gently pass,
  And full salvation flows.

3 If e'er I go astray,
  He doth my soul reclaim;   [way,
  And guides me, in His own right
  For His most holy name.

141. HAPPY DAY. L. M.

1 O happy day, that fixed my choice
  On Thee, my Saviour and my God!
  Well may this glowing heart rejoice,
  And tell its raptures all abroad.

CHO.—Happy day, happy day,
  When Jesus washed my sins away;
  He taught me how to watch and pray,
  And live rejoicing every day;
  Happy day, happy day.
  When Jesus washed my sins away.

SELECTED HYMNS.

2 Now rest, my long-divided heart;
Fixed on this blissful centre, rest;
Nor ever from thy Lord depart,
With Him of every good possessed. Cho.

3 High heaven, that heard the solemn vow,
That vow renewed shall daily hear,
Till in life's latest hour I bow,
And bless in death a bond so dear. Cho.

---

142. CROSS AND CROWN. C.M.

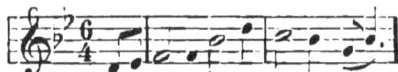

1 Must Jesus bear the cross alone,
And all the world go free!
No; there's a cross for every one,
And there's a cross for me.

2 How happy are the saints above,
Who once went sorrowing here;
But now they taste unmingled love
And joy without a tear.

3 The consecrated cross I'll bear,
Till death shall set me free;
And then go home, my crown to wear,
For there's a crown for me.

---

143. OLIVET. 6s & 4s.

1 My faith looks up to Thee,
Thou Lamb of Calvary,
Saviour divine:
Now hear me while I pray,
Take all my guilt away,
O let me from this day
Be wholly Thine.

2 May thy rich grace impart
Strength to my fainting heart
My zeal inspire;
As Thou hast died for me,
O may my love to Thee
Pure, warm and changeless be—
A living fire.

---

144. BALERMA. C.M.

1 Come, humble sinner, in whose breast
A thousand thoughts revolve,
Come, with your guilt and fear oppressed,
And make this last resolve:

2 I'll go to Jesus, though my sin
Like mountains round me close;
I know His courts, I'll enter in,
Whatever may oppose.

3 Prostrate I'll lie before His throne,
And there my guilt confess,
I'll tell Him I'm a wretch undone
Without His sov'reign grace.

---

4 Perhaps He will admit my plea,
Perhaps will hear my prayer;
But, if I perish, I will pray,
And perish only there.

5 I can but perish if I go—
I am resolved to try;
For if I stay away I know
I shall forever die.

REV. EDMUND JONES.

---

145. AZMON. C. M.

1 O for a closer walk with God,
A calm and heavenly frame,
A light to shine upon the road
That leads me to the Lamb.

2 Where is the blessedness I knew
When first I saw the Lord?
Where is the soul refreshing view
Of Jesus and His word?

3 What peaceful hours I once enjoyed!
How sweet their mem'ry still!
But they have left an aching void
The world can never fill.

4 Return, O holy Dove, return,
Sweet messenger of rest;
I hate the sins that made Thee mourn,
And drove Thee from my breast.

---

146. DORRANCE. 8s & 7s.

1 Take my heart, O Father, take it;
Make and keep it all Thine own;
Let Thy Spirit melt and break it,
This proud heart of sin and stone.

2 Father, make it pure and lowly,
Fond of peace, and far from strife;
Turning from the paths unholy
Of this vain and sinful life.

3 Ever let Thy grace surround it;
Strengthen it with power divine,
Till Thy cords of love have bound it;
Make it to be wholly Thine.

ANON.

---

147. LEBANON. S. M. D.

1 I was a wandering sheep;
I did not love the fold;
I did not love my Shepherd's voice;
I would not be controlled.

(124)

SELECTED HYMNS.

I was a wayward child ;
I did not love my home :
I did not love my Father's voice ;
I loved afar to roam.

2 The Shepherd sought his sheep,
The Father sought his child ;
They followed me o'er vale and hill,
O'er deserts waste and wild.
They found me nigh to death.
Famished, and faint, and lone.
They bound me with the bands of love,
They saved the wandering one.

3 Jesus my shepherd is ;
'Twas He that loved my soul ;
'Twas He that washed me in His blood.
'Twas He that made me whole ;
'Twas He that sought the lost.
That found the wandering sheep ;
'Twas He that brought me to the fold,
'Tis He that still doth keep.

DR. H. BONAR.

148. UXBRIDGE. L. M.

1 Lord I am Thine, entirely Thine.
Purchased and saved by blood divine ;
With full consent Thine would I be,
And own thy sov'reign right to me.

1 Grant one poor sinner more a place
Among the children of Thy grace ;
A wretched sinner, lost from God,
But ransomed by Immanuel's blood.

4 Thine would I live, Thine would I die ;
Be thine through all eternity :
The vow is passed beyond repeal,
And now I set the solemn seal.

REV. SAMUEL DAVIES.

149. STEPHENS. C. M.

1 O for a heart to praise my God,
A heart from sin set free ;
A heart that always feels Thy blood,
So freely spilt for me.

2 A heart resign'd, submissive, meek,
My great Redeemer's throne ;
Where only Christ is heard to speak,
Where Jesus reigns alone.

3 O for a lowly, contrite heart,
Believing, true and clean ;
Which neither life nor death can part
From Him that dwells within.

4 A heart in every thought renew'd,
And full of love divine ;
Perfect and right, and pure, and good,
A copy, Lord, of Thine.

REV. CHAS. WESLEY.

150. HORTON. 7s.

1 Come, saith Jesus' sacred voice,
Come and make my paths your choice ;
I will guide you to your home ;
Weary pilgrim, hither come.

2 Hither come, for here is found
Balm for every bleeding wound ;
Peace which ever shall endure,
Rest eternal, sacred, sure.

MRS. A. L. BARBAULD, 1825.

151. STATE STREET. S. M.

1 My God, my life, my love,
To Thee, to Thee I call :
I cannot live if Thou remove,
For Thou art all in all.

2 Thy shining grace can cheer
This dungeon where I dwell ;
'Tis paradise when Thou art here
If Thou depart, 'tis hell.

3 The smilings of Thy face,
How amiable they are !
'Tis heaven to rest in Thine embrace,
And nowhere else but there.

REV. ISAAC WATTS.

152. WINDHAM. L. M.

1 Show pity, Lord, O Lord, forgive ;
Let a repenting rebel live ;
Are not Thy mercies large and free ?
May not a sinner trust in Thee ?

2 My crimes are great, but don't surpass
The power and glory of Thy grace :
Great God, Thy nature hath no bound—
So let Thy pard'ning love be found.

3 O wash my soul from every sin,
And make my guilty conscience clean ;
Here on my heart the burden lies,
And past offences pain my eyes.

4 My lips with shame my sins confess,
Against Thy law, against Thy grace ;
Lord, should Thy judgments grow severe,
I am condemned, but Thou art clear.

OLD HUNDRED. L. M.

Praise God, from whom all blessings flow ;
Praise Him all creatures here below :
Praise Him above, ye heavenly host ;
Praise Father, Son and Holy Ghost.

INDEX.

Titles in Small Caps.—First Lines in Roman.

(126)

INDEX.

INDEX.

www.ingramcontent.com/pod-product-compliance
Lightning Source LLC
Chambersburg PA
CBHW030625270326
41927CB00007B/1302